LOST ON
BAY STREET

Also by Alex Doulis

Take Your Money and Run
My Blue Haven
The Bond's Revenge
Tackling the Taxman

Alex Doulis

LOST ON BAY STREET

I Came,

I Saw,

I Almost

Conquered

BASTIAN BOOKS

Published by Bastian Books
www.bastianbooks.com
Toronto, Canada
A division of Bastian Publishing Services Ltd.

Distributed by Publishers Group Canada
www.pgcbooks.ca

ISBN 978-0-9782221-3-0

Cataloguing in Publication data available from Library and Archives Canada

Cover design: Angel Guerra, Archetype
Text design and typesetting: Kinetics Design
www.kdbooks.ca

Printed and bound by Tri-Graphic Printing Ltd.

To all who have experienced a loss on Bay Street,

the avenue of Canadian corporate capitalism.

For most the loss will have been monetary,

but there is a cadre who lost their integrity, morality,

and in some cases personal freedom on Bay Street.

Most in this latter group have been released from our jails,

but to those of you still there,

my best wishes for a speedy release.

Contents

Introduction

During my pre–Bay Street years, I was a field geologist. I wandered through the mountains of the coast range, the deserts of the interior, and the tundra of the north. I can't remember ever not knowing where I was or where I was going. Even on the coast of Alaska, where the sun is seldom seen and weird magnetic anomalies distract your compass, I never felt lost. Furthermore, I always knew what my objectives were: map this area's geology, determine whether there are economic minerals in the environs, and prove their worth, if any. And whenever I worked with a helper, guide, or companion, I had complete trust in them because we were all pursuing the same thing.

Working in Toronto on Bay Street, in the financial jungle of Canada, seldom offered me the same clarity. So many things distracted the moral compass that it was difficult for me to maintain my way. And as for anyone who could help me reach my objectives, forget about it. I had been taught most of my bush lore by Pinky Foster and Tom McCready, aboriginal Canadians. Pinky taught me how to work in the desert and Tom how to survive in the swamp. However, I met no aboriginals in the deserts or swamps of the investment industry. How could this be? They had been trading furs for smoked fish among themselves long before we brought our trading houses to these shores.

In leaving the bush for Bay Street, I should have learned from history of the clash that occurs when geology meets finance. Whole television series – *Deadwood*, for example – have been based on that result. In this book, as on the flickering blue screen, there are more villains than heroes.

1

But what is this phenomenon called Bay Street? Much has been written about the side of the street on which deception, deceit, greed, and avarice stroll hand in hand. That is actually the sunny side. The shady side, where all the moral signposts have been burned to provide heat for the boiler rooms, and morality consists of not getting caught stoking the fires, is where I'll take you in this book.

It never starts out like this. Stockbroking firms begin with the objective of helping investors to exchange their current shareholdings for something else or dispose of them completely at a reasonable cost. The underwriting side is there to allow companies to raise money for their development or expansion at the lowest possible cost.

But there is so damned much money passing by, why not take a little more out for me or us or the whole extended clan? When the trading side had fixed commissions, the guaranteed income they supplied to the industry's insiders effectively lowered the gains of the investors. In the era of the exclusive underwriting syndicates, exclusivity increased the costs facing the corporations seeking capital and paid the golf-club fees for the investment industry.

When you have a gravy train, which is what the investment business was until the 1980s, you certainly don't want ethnics to enter the industry. Their kind of thinking might bring about change. (It wasn't just the WASPs in Canada who operated this way. The same attitude was adopted by many of the Jewish firms in New York.) One former partner of mine of Irish descent had astounded his father by actually getting a job on the trading desk at Wood Gundy in Toronto. Imagine – an Irishman working in the brokerage business. Better count the silverware.

Brainpower is not determined by creed, and some of the firms that wanted to get an advantage over their confrères decided that putting a few ethnics into the support area of the business couldn't do any harm. They didn't realize, however, that it was the old "camel's head in the tent" syndrome: You allow the head in, and the next thing you know the whole beast has taken over the tent.

As a result of all this, the shady side of Bay Street actually saw a lot of sun in the 1980s, and fortunes were lost and made. The mansions got new owners and the clubs new members. Are the investors any better off today? Tyco, Hollinger, HealthSouth, front running, insider trading. No, it's just a different group lining their pockets in different ways, though still at your, the investor's, expense.

So where will I be taking you in this mixed tale of loss and triumph? The early pages of this book cover my rough and ready years as a young geologist, working that lucrative seam between mining and investing, mostly in British Columbia. The book then goes on to describe my attempts to break into the holy of holies of the firm for which I toiled, A.E. Ames & Co.

Next comes the period after I was rebuffed by the priests who guarded the inner sanctum of Ames, when I took up residence at Gordon Capital, This was when the fun really began: when the ethnics almost took control of the corporate suite.

Lost on Bay Street is replete with a cast of colourful and often brilliant characters, including Murray Pezim, Bob Buchan, Peter Hyland, Conrad Black, Vincent Harbinson, and Peter Munk. It describes the "stages" on which these talented people played their parts, major brokerage companies such as A.E. Ames, Gordon Capital, Deacon Hodgson, and McNeil Mantha. And it documents the revolution and evolution of the financial industry, in which my fellow ethnic financial outsiders at Gordon were instrumental in getting rid of rigged-commission schedules and closed-underwriting syndicates. The howls of lost privilege may be heard up and down the Bay Street Canyon to this day.

Writing about the high points and low points of a life spent on Bay Street and squeezing them between two covers has been an experience with its ... well, with its high and low points. The task was not easy but has been immensely fulfilling, taking me back to the heady days of the Toronto Stock Exchange from the 1960s to the turn of the century. It was an experience that I enjoyed, for the most part, though I still sport some bruises from the more treacherous events involved.

The events that follow are tinctured by my own physical and psychological struggles, courtesy of all the fun and games mentioned. Although the events span the past forty-five years, I remember them perfectly. Some of the actual conversations involved are also clearly etched in my mind. This is the way it was.

I

GETTING MY HANDS DIRTY

1

Different Jungle, Fewer Mosquitoes

I didn't want to become a stockbroker, and in the strictest sense I didn't: I was classified as an analyst. However, in spite of what you may hear to the contrary, all back-office support functions in the investment industry are dedicated to sales. In other words, I was part of the team to get you to buy something. Without sales, there are no commissions, bonus cheques, or partnership payouts.

So how did I get to Bay Street? It is a strange tale.

My life was a happy one as a geologist, primarily on the left coast. I worked in Alaska, the Yukon, and British Columbia, and then inland, in Utah. I met interesting people. I mean *really* interesting, like remittance men from between the world wars, cashiered officers, and hermits. Mind you, the investment business had its fair share of scoundrels, as well, but there was no one you could point to on that street and be thrilled to meet.

My favourite remittance man was Godfrey, a tall, imposing Brit reduced by age to a shuffling gait. I would often see him in the early mornings. I was working out of Keremeos, B.C., a dusty desert town in the south-central part of the province where it was good planning to start working early in the day and quit before the heat became intolerable. Godfrey's kin had sent him off to Canada for an undisclosed peccadillo, intending that he oversee the development of some mining claims belonging to the clan.

Godfrey confided in me one night that he had guessed something wasn't right when his ticket to Canada was without a return portion and the mine he was sent to oversee turned out to be a patch of ground with a trench cut in one corner. The choice facing him was to somehow return to England, its ghastly climate, his appalling family, and the consequences of his undisclosed transgression or remain in Canada and enjoy the dry desert climate and his monthly cheque. Godfrey picked the dry desert air, which was a balm to his ravaged lungs, which had been gassed during World War I.

This was my first encounter with the dangers inherent in finance and investing. Godfrey's cheques were in pounds sterling. This was a great currency at the end of World War I, but after that it was subject to continuing devaluations until the man was left in penury by the time I met him, in 1961. This was my introduction to the effects of price fluctuations of commodities, whether they be currencies or metals.

Then there were the mining claims. It was not uncommon in the interwar years for a confidence man to sell Canadian moose pasture (in this case a rattlesnake pasture) to overseas investors, just as Florida land salesmen sold swamps to the unsuspecting American investors. Godfrey's family had been duped into buying some mining property sight unseen on the basis of a few assay reports. In subsequent years I saw the same process being repeated on the stock exchanges, though instead of one victim there were thousands.

That was just my preliminary skirmish with the investing addiction. It got worse. After spending the summer of 1961 in the oppressive heat of the B.C. desert, I found winter employment in the Highland Valley copper belt of the same province. The snow and cold of the valley are legendary. My job was to lay out an access road to some mining claims across the valley from the producing Bethlehem Copper mine. Bulldozing the road revealed a fifty-foot-wide exposure of high-grade copper mineralization. This would obviously be very beneficial to the company and its owners, so what was a young geologist to do? Well, immediately find a phone and call Vancouver, of course.

Today you would call company management. Instead I called my broker and bought ten thousand shares of Peel Resources (the owners of the claims) at the opening of the Vancouver Exchange that morning. After my order had been confirmed at $0.17 per share, I called my boss, Neil McDermid, and told him of the company's great good fortune. The shares closed that night at $0.48 per share with no news having been released. Others as well informed as I had thought the shares worth a "flutter." It didn't require the efforts of the anti-terror squad to figure out who was raiding the exchange.

It was my boss and his nearest and dearest. They, of course, had to tell their buddies, and the next thing you knew, the share price was looking like a NASA launch.

I had managed to get some samples for assay on the noon bus to Vancouver, as well as piece of rock the size of a person's head for Neil to put on his desk. This I was more than happy to do because by the end of the week the shares I had purchased at $0.17 were trading at over a dollar. When the shares popped to over $1.50, I knew Neil had the assay results, though I still could find no announcement of them in the business or mining press. Once again Neil and his friends were in the market well in advance of sharing the results with the public. When the results did come out, the stock traded in large volume but closed below the $1.50 level it had attained. As always, realization didn't meet expectations. This phenomenon was described by Oscar Wilde when he was asked for his thoughts on Niagara Falls. "The second greatest disappointment of American brides," he said.

Meanwhile, I was still out in the frozen hills with my bulldozer, trying to determine the surface extent of this bounty. I moved the machine fifty feet to the south and encountered the vein again. This time, however, it was only twenty feet wide. I concluded that I had crossed the vein in my first encounter at other than ninety degrees, giving it a greater than actual width. Being true to the geologist's ever-optimistic code, I knew that the bonanza lay to the north, not the south. I started uncovering the northern extension, but it, too, was small, and I realized that my find was just a tiny lens of high-grade ore and probably uneconomic.

I phoned my boss – after having sold my ten thousand shares at $1.48 – and told him my conclusions. The shares closed that night at just over $1 and then eventually drifted back to the $0.35 level. The deposit never proved to be of worth, but I was wealthier by $13,000.

However, being a novice, I was half as rich as I should have been. I didn't know about short selling, where an investor sells shares he doesn't own with the intent of buying them at a later date and lower price to fulfill his contract. I should have sold twenty thousand shares at $1.48: the ten thousand I owned and the ten thousand "short" that I could have easily financed with my concurrent sale of the shares I owned.

Don't start with the tsk, tsk. This was 1962 and here were no insider-trading rules. One of the benefits of being a geologist was that you got the first shot at the trading blotter as recompense for being out there among the mosquitoes or on the frozen waste. Almost the first shot. We were being beat out of first place by the other workers. Some drillers were making fortunes by looking at the core as it came out of the drills and trading shares on the basis of whether the rock was shiny or not. When the company owners tried to stop that practice by disallowing the core-recovery tubes to be emptied in front of the drillers, the workers weighed the sealed core boxes instead. A heavy box meant a good hole: the rock in the sealed box could be deduced to contain heavy metallic minerals.

On one job I was on I saw the drill helper roaring down the mountain-side in his pickup truck. I ran out my core shack to see if I could assist in whatever calamity had occurred at the site, but he drove past me in a swirl of dust and the moaning of tortured tires. I concluded that the storm and fury must have been over the need for a tool of some kind back in town. When he returned, I flagged him down, fearing that the missing equipment might have been manufactured in a brewery. Oh no, the man said. During the drilling the re-circulating return water from the drill hole had turned black, indicating the presence of metallic minerals at the drill face. He had just driven to town to phone in the crew members' purchase orders for our company's shares to their respective brokers.

What was a geologist to do? I called my broker before even going out to the site. I knew that the drillers, when they finished their shift, would hit the local bar and soon everyone in town would know and the share price would be on the climb. If you think that's despicable, it gets worse.

As a result of my good fortune, I had sold my MG sports car and bought a more exotic vehicle, a Morgan. I was sure I was about to become a very wealthy man. There was nothing to stop me as long as I was at the drill site when the water turned black. There was a golden, copper, or zinc goose out there ready to be plucked. A few more years of being frozen, mosquito bitten, and rain soaked and I would retire to Cap Ferrat on the French Riviera. The stock market was a surefire road to infinite riches for a drill-site geologist such as I.

I had taken some time off from my role as a serious inside trader to kick around Vancouver and in the evenings entertain students of St. Paul's Hospital School of Nursing. My sojourns in the city can only be described as idyllic. I lived in a mansion in Shaugnessey, Vancouver's equivalent to Toronto's Rosedale or San Francisco's Knob Hill. No, I didn't own the palace; I was renting one of its eight bedrooms from Milty, a mining lawyer. In the evenings, when we were all ordering out for Chinese and cracking open a few beers, Milty would ask the most recent arrivals to partake of his hospitality how things were going out in the bush. If there was any mention of a fresh staking of claims or of moving a drill or other equipment onto a property, Milty was up early the next day pounding on the doors of the mining company involved, offering his services as Vancouver's greatest mining lawyer.

The only time Milty relaxed was on Saturday nights, when he would invite student nurses or Australian practising nurses for party night. There was an apartment building on Thurlow Street in downtown Vancouver where Australian Sheilas on their way around the world would put up while in Vancouver. Most of them were nurses, which is how Milty got his entry to the nursing schools. He had met some of the Australians, invited them to the mansion, and they in turn had encouraged the students to come. I soon determined that Australian girls, as a result of some genetic quirk, had an immense tolerance for beer. I switched to nursing students.

During the days I would frequent a downtown White Spot coffee shop where the local mining fraternity gathered to tell each other lies. Once, while I was being told by a promoter about the richest gold mine never found at Atlin Lake in Northern B.C. and how just a few thousand of my easily acquired dollars should be put into his company, which was sure to find that elusive deposit, the king of promoters sat down beside me. He asked if I was doing anything, to which I replied that I was in rest and recuperation mode but could be bought. Back at his office, the conversation went like this.

"Axel, if you have nothing on, how about some core logging?"

Now, core logging is incredibly dull. You look at the drill cores lying in trays brought in from the rigs and record the geology. If there are metallic mineralized sections, you have these split in half and return a semicircular piece to the core box while sending the other half to an assay office to determine the metal content. The benefits are that aside from the paltry salary paid, you get to see the core first and any geologist worth his degree can estimate roughly what the assay results will be. So after a day's logging, you arrange to take the split sections for transport to the assay office and call your stockbroker. Another day at the office, another tax-free score. (Prior to 1972 there was no capital-gains tax in Canada.)

How tedious, how enriching!

You may also be wondering about this man calling me Axel. It was a name that had been created by rearranging the letters in my first name to give it a more woodsy flavour. Sort of like Marion Morrison having his name changed to John Wayne.

Murray Pezim was at the top of the heap. He could separate a speculator from his hard-earned cash so effortlessly that it seemed predestined he should have the chump's bucks. I remember his being almost in tears as he admitted to a speculator in one of his failed mining schemes how, as he put it: "We all lost on this one, Jack. But I am going to make it up to you. I am going to sell you some of my own cheap shares in my new venture so you can ride this with me. We'll get you back everything you lost and more." Eventually the chumps gave up on possibly making it on Murray's next venture. But the crop of suckers was a crop that never failed. There were always new greed-driven goofs lined up at Murray's door. The essence of his pitch was the "we." He placed himself in the same boat as the money-losing speculators, though his money was never actually at risk.

To be asked to log core for the king was to be in a prime position. Murray could make a share price shine with a minimum of real news.

"Sure," I said. "Where is it and what are you paying?"

"It's near Kamloops and I am paying a thousand a day plus expenses."

I couldn't believe what I was hearing. In the 1960s you were lucky to get $250 a day for a short-term project. This one had to be really short. Also, I could tell that this didn't smell right. It struck me that for that kind of pay I wouldn't be looking at core that Murray was entitled to see.

"Whose core am I logging?"

It turned out to belong to a colourful ex-football player who was using his name recognition as an entry to the mining-promotion business. When Murray told me the area, Kamloops, I knew exactly which company was doing the drilling. They had drilled a couple of long holes in the vicinity of an old copper mine and had encountered encouraging results in the first two holes. The market players believed, based on the amount of time elapsed, that at a minimum three holes had gone unreported after the initial drilling. The share price continued to climb, indicating, again, that the insiders were withholding the results until they had filled their hats with cheap shares. How typical.

Murray was not so sure. His thesis was that the ex-athlete had been hit on the head enough times by opposing fullbacks in that era of low-tech football helmets that there must have been some loss of reasoning power. Murray's belief was that the man and his lads were not encountering anything encouraging in their latest drilling, which was why there was no news coming out. As long as the shares inched upward on no news, the speculators were optimistic. If a slow sinking of the shares started, a day would come when there would be an almost instant collapse. Murray had to know what was in that core.

There was more to the story. Murray had just been party to an amazing flameout where a company he had promoted went from pennies to $7 a share to pennies in a matter of weeks. Even the brain-dead directors of the Vancouver Stock Exchange were startled out of their somnambulance: some of their firm's floor traders had been left holding a significant amount of Murray's now worthless stock.

There were rumours that Murray had shorted his own deal. He wasn't about to be looked on with favour if he tried to float another deal so soon after his last triumph and the market's sorrow. So he decided to make some money off of other people's promotions. He knew that the vast majority of the mining deals on the Vancouver exchange were either crooked or worthless. Even he was aware that the odds of success in real mining exploration were 140 to 1. By being on the short side of a deal, you invariably won. But the canyons of Vancouver's financial district were littered with the lucre of those who had shorted a $5 stock and lost their nerve as the stock went to $8 on its way to $0.05. If you had just sold shares short at $5 and everybody was telling you this was the big one (otherwise it wouldn't be going up), you would either fold and buy some more or hold onto your own convictions and your wallet. Murray didn't have convictions of any kind (although a situation on the Toronto Exchange had brought censure). He wanted facts.

"Murray, what you are talking about isn't exactly ethical," I said with a touch of sanctimony. "It may even be criminal."

"For god's sake, kid, look at what's going on," he said. "Those sleazebags are withholding information that the shareholders have a right to know. If they're not going to release the information, then someone has to obtain it and put it out into the marketplace. We're doing a public service by keeping the market honest."

"What are you going to do, Murray? Issue a press release?"

"Don't be cute, kid. If we know what's in the core boxes, then by association the market will know. This is a form of investment research."

Now I knew why Murray was known as king of the promoters. He could sell anything. He had just sold me. It was obvious that the market would know if the results were good or bad at Western Canadian Copper on the basis of whether Murray bought a hundred thousand shares or short-sold that amount. Whichever way Murray went on the stock, he would be sure to tell his nearest and dearest after he had his position. Then everyone else would jump on the bandwagon and the parade would come marching home to capital-gains heaven.

"Murray, they shoot people for pilfering from placer sluice boxes," I said. "What do they do to people who tamper with core? Throw them out of helicopters?"

Little did I know that I had just conceived of a method to be used thirty years later when the geologist Michael de Guzman was thrown out of a helicopter during the Bre-X scandal for just such tampering. It was also my first foray into mining-investment analysis. I was about to become a mining analyst.

"Look, kid, you'll be in out and real quick," Murray said. "I had someone fly over the site with a light plane. The core shack is between the campsite and the drills. It's about a quarter of a mile from the core shack to either the drill or the camp. We'll fly in with a chopper to within five miles of the shack. We'll land at dusk and walk in. The logging is done at night and we'll be out the next morning."

I was incredulous. Overweight Murray would be by my side? He didn't trust me? What was up?

"You're coming with me?" I asked.

"No, kid. It's just a manner of speaking. But I'll be with you all the way."

"Murray, here's the deal," I said. "You pay me $2,000 and all expenses. I get $1,200 up front, a $200 expense advance, and $1,000 retainer. I get the second $1,000 upon return to Vancouver and any expenses owing. Don't try to negotiate because you and I both know you need this desperately."

He agreed but forgot to specify what would turn out to be some very important details.

I drove to Kamloops and found the waiting helicopter. I landed behind a small hill within an hour's walk to the core shack. I had learned that the drills were working two twelve-hour shifts and concluded that shift change would be around 7 or 8 p.m. I heard the drill and the pumps stop and then restart an hour later, so I knew the second shift was at work and it was time for me to begin.

The core-shack door was constructed of two-by-four timbers laid on edge. The lock was about the size of a railway lock. There was no way I could get through the door. The sides, however, were different. They consisted of three-eighths-inch plywood held on with roofing nails. Brilliant! I used my rock hammer and knife to carefully remove sheet after sheet and pull the five-foot-long core trays out. With my miner's lamp on and clipboard in hand, I was ready to log. The trays were carefully labeled 62-1, 62-2, and on, in sequence. I knew what the results of holes 1 and 2 were. They had been released to the public. It was the subsequent holes that I was being paid to log.

I could find none of the geology common to British Columbia – large low-grade copper deposits of the Highland Valley type – nor could I find much in the way of copper mineralization in the core, and this was supposed to be a copper find. The best section I found containing copper was in hole 5, and it was only twelve feet long. I "eyeballed" the grade at less than two percent copper. About as valuable as a politician's promise.

I took a small piece of the core from the mineralized section for assay. I waited until the sun began to glow on the hills to the east before beginning my trek. I had spent the time before daybreak cleaning up all traces of my presence, to the extent of even sweeping away my boot prints in the sand with tree boughs. I still had visions of bungee diving from a helicopter without the bungee cord. There were also other considerations. For this information to be valuable, nobody – particularly the promoters of this company – could know I had it.

The helicopter picked me up at 9 a.m., as arranged. I arrived in Kamloops as the market was opening in Vancouver. I had $15,000 in my brokerage account and, being a little more market savvy by this time, shorted $30,000 worth of stock at around $5 a share. After breakfast I checked into a motel, called the nursing school, and caught six hours' sleep before heading down the Fraser Canyon Highway to Vancouver.

The next morning I stopped at the assay office with my purloined piece of core and asked that it be examined for copper, molybdenum, gold, and silver. By the time I arrived at Murray's office, the trading for the day had begun and I saw, on his personal ticker, that the stock I had shorted was still holding its price.

"Well?" he asked.

"It's a bust. There's nothing there and the setting isn't typical of the Highland Valley open pits. They should have stopped drilling after hole 4."

"They couldn't. They're trying to get C.M. Oliver to underwrite an issue," he said.

Now it was getting complicated. If the C.M. Oliver brokerage house underwrote an issue at around $4.50, they would try to support the price until they blew out as much stock as possible to the public. Was Murray going to sucker C.M. Oliver into buying his short sales? That would be dangerous, because Oliver would never do a deal with him in the future. Was he trying to curry favour at Oliver's? It was hard to know for sure, but obviously the prospective underwriting was playing a major part in the deal. I was starting to worry about my $30,000 short position in the stock when Murray popped the question I knew would come.

"Hey, kid, did you get some samples?"

"Sure did, Murray, and they're already at the assay office. I'll bring you the results as soon as I have them."

Of course he went ballistic when he heard that the he would not be the first person to view the results. Murray had made a big mistake. When we set up the deal, he had not demanded that the samples be delivered to him.

That afternoon I could see Murray's hand in the market as the stock-trading volume started to pick up. Sometimes it moved up, only to fall back. His objective was size. He had to get as big a position sold as possible before the floor fell out from under the price. So he was both a seller and a buyer, giving the appearance of market activity, all the while building his short position.

The day after I gave Murray the assay results, the shares collapsed. A couple of the backers of the company were on the verge of bankruptcy, but Murray had made a bundle and won some friends at C.M. Oliver.

Some people I relate this incident to are aghast. Where were my morals in having "front run" my employer? Well, wait just a minute. I took the risks in a dangerous, probably illegal venture and you're asking me to be a Boy Scout? As far as I was concerned, once you crossed the moral line with others, you had no obligations to anyone but yourself.

My short proved very bountiful, because the price I covered at was less than fifty cents. The shares I bought for $0.47 I had sold at $5, all six thousand of them. Do the math, as they say. I was looking at trading in the Morgan for a Jaguar. My tailor said I should keep the Morgan and buy the Jag for formal wear. It made sense.

But unbeknownst to me there were storm clouds on the eastern horizon. Drilling had begun on a property near Timmins, Ontario, that would change the lives of all field geologists.

And others were having difficulty with car brands.

2

The Ford Rolls Royce

REMEMBER Jack who lost money with Murray at the outset? Jack Howard was an insurance agent in Vancouver. He had his own agency and lived in a nice house in West Vancouver.

Jack had a client, Hans Bor, who was a prospector. The prospector offered to pay him the insurance premiums on his Land Rover in shares of the Rio Plata Silver Company. In those days Land Rovers were bush vehicles designed to run forever, though all the bits like windscreens, doors, and anything else bolted on, fell off. Jack took the bait and then encouraged all his friends and clients to buy the over-the-counter shares.

Jack followed the age-old dictum, "Invest then investigate." A very sound business procedure in some eyes. But he was not going to take the time off from his busy schedule to go up to Mayo, Yukon Territory, and then take forty miles of bush road into the claims, so he asked me to go up to look at the property, which was next to one owned by a company called Peso Silver. This latter property had been the object of massive funding and was undergoing major exploration.

The Rio Plata property was in Dublin Gulch, an area that was being placer mined. I obtained permission from the placer miners to look at the rejects and gold from their sluice boxes. I found no large pieces of silver ore but did find, interestingly, cassiterite, a tin ore. The gold that was being recovered was very fine and the pieces well rounded. It had come from far away. The cassiterite pebbles were also round. A bonanza on the Rio Plata claims was unlikely.

I went to the Peso Silver camp and found that they had conducted an airborne survey over most of the area and had acquired all the claims showing any sign of promise.

When I returned to Vancouver, I informed Jack that Bor had done a location-staking job. That's where you stake claims near an existing deposit in the hopes that whatever was on those claims, including stock-market action, extended to what you had staked. But unlike in real estate, location in mining doesn't guarantee success. Jack was crestfallen and vowed never to go into a mining venture again unless he controlled it.

A couple of years later I returned to Vancouver and met Jack downtown at the White Spot coffee shop. He asked me if I knew anything about a company called Anvil Mines, headed up by Aaro Aho, a well-known Canadian geologist of Finnish extraction. I admitted my ignorance of the property, though mentioned that some of my old school buddies had asked me to work up there for cash and shares. I was already overstocked on worthless shares, so I had demurred.

Jack admitted to having bought a hundred thousand treasury shares at $0.25 and was now being offered a further hundred thousand at $0.50 from the treasury.

I asked him if he was on the board.

"No."

"What happened to your pledge to be in control?"

Jack launched into a monologue about the merits of the property, but I cut him short. In any case, he took me home for dinner where his wife, Marilyn, was happy to see me once again. Sort of. She was incensed with Jack's forays into mining speculation and considered anyone involved in the industry to be a Neanderthal con man. The only talk of mining that night regarded out-of-town jobs that might be of interest to me.

A year later I stopped in at the White Spot and encountered Jack again. I had just got back to Vancouver after a winter of salvaging an old gold mine in the Yukon and making some good money. Although I liked working as a geologist alone or with one other person, a winter in constant company didn't appeal to me. I determined that I was probably a loner and stayed in exploration instead of moving into production.

"Jack, if Marilyn hears that you're hanging around this place, she'll have your guts for garters," I said. "She's come over to the dark side. By the way, the Anvil Mining thing paid off big. Aaro's a millionaire, as are some of your old school chums who worked with him."

As for Anvil, I was crushed to know I had missed working on what had become a major zinc producer in the Yukon. Jack cheered me up by asking me home to see Marilyn and have dinner. My car was still in storage, so we drove up in his. When we arrived at his house, I noticed a new Ford Mustang in the driveway. It was 1964 and they were very popular and difficult to obtain.

"Hey, nice Mustang, Jack. You must know somebody to have got a hold of one."

"It's not a Mustang. It's a Rolls Royce."

"What am I missing? I don't see a Roller."

"That gray two-door is in reality a Rolls Royce. It just looks like a Mustang."

"Okay, what are you trying to tell me?"

"Marilyn was pestering me about getting her a new car. So I went to see Jimmy Pattison and gave him six thousand shares of Anvil for the Mustang. At the time, the shares were about a buck, so everybody was happy. Today the shares are $16. That makes the Mustang worth about $96,000, or the price of a Rolls-Royce Silver Ghost. It's probably best to not say anything to Marilyn about the car. It's still a sensitive issue."

What Jack had done was trade some of his "lettered" Anvil stock for a car with the legendary B.C. financier, who was then just starting his career. When you bought treasury shares from a company as a private placement (an issue not available to the public generally), the shares had a one-year hold period. That meant that the buyer could not trade them on the exchange but was required to hold them for a period of a year from the purchase date. There was no prohibition against selling the shares privately, though the legend on the stock remained and the new owner was faced with holding the shares until the legend expired before they could be exchange traded.

The hold period offered two risks: first, that the intrinsic value of the shares would fall before the hold period expired, and second, that when the hold period ended, there would be a rush for the door, making it difficult to offload the shares. Pattison took the risk. I guess that's why he's a multi-millionaire today. He was a good judge of risk.

3

It's Not That Easy

BY now you may have concluded that the mining industry was the man-on-the-street's route to instant riches. Well, it was for the Hearsts, Guggenheims, and Timminses of this world, but for the rest of us it was a hard slog. To begin with, most people believed that when they bought their little homestead, they owned it all. Not true. They owned only the top few meters. Everything below that belonged to the state. Let me give you an example.

There you are at your summer property on the lake sitting on the veranda sipping a tall cool one. You hear some noise and turn to see an individual wearing heavy lace-up boots, stained and dirty khaki trousers, a khaki shirt with what looks like long underwear underneath (even though it's summer), and a hand lens hung around his neck. Local colour, you conclude.

"Boy are you lucky," says he. "I've just found a diamond pipe right behind your outhouse."

What he fails to tell you is that you don't own the diamond pipe. Remember the plastic ribbon around the trees and posts with their tops sharpened to look like pyramids that you saw when you drove up in the spring? Those were mining-claim stakes. Someone had staked the mineral rights underlying your property and now owned the rights to the prospective diamond pipe. If the pipe is explored and developed, the best you can hope for would be compensation for your discomfort.

Very few realize that they are only acquiring the surface rights when they purchase a piece of land. The mineral rights in the first instance belong to the state and in the second instance may have been passed from the state to some commercial entity. Much of the mineral rights in central and western Canada were given to either the Hudson Bay Company (hence the old Hudson's Bay Oil and Gas Company and Hudson Bay Mining and Smelting Co.) or the Canadian Pacific Railway (exploited by the old Canadian Pacific Oil and Gas Company).

You can well imagine the difficulty this presents to the guys in the dirty khaki trousers, the geologists.

When first confronted with the fact that he does not own the mineral rights underlying his property, the typical land owner goes into disbelief. When he is shown the pertinent sections of the provincial mining act the emotion changes to rage while uttering something like, "Get off my property. You're trespassing."

The geologist then flips to the pages of the Mineral Act describing access to mineral claims. This is usually along the lines of allowing a minimum fourteen-foot right of way to the nearest public thoroughfare. At this point the geologist starts to run for his truck, knowing it's going to take the landowner a full week to cool down and accept his cruel fate.

There are, however, diabolical people who don't capitulate with dignity. I encountered one such in Southern British Columbia, near the town of Oliver.

I was on the hunt for molybdenum, a steel additive (yes, children, there was a molybdenum boom in the 1960s, not just in 2007) for which B.C. is well known. I had seen a claim map in the mine recorder's office showing two old "Crown-granted" mineral claims dating from the mid-1800s up in the mountains west of Oliver. These are claims on which sufficient exploration funds have been spent that title can be held by paying an annual fee. Even when the fees haven't been paid, the claims can be reactivated. These claims had been explored for copper only, because in the 1800s molybdenum was worthless. But in B.C., where there is copper there often is molybdenum.

Along with my horse Headlight and a packhorse I spent a day getting up to the claims, which still had remnants of the last snows. Where the old-timers had excavated and tunneled, the showings were spectacular in molybdenum but middling in copper, which is what they were pursuing. I took some samples, did some mapping, and a week later headed down the mountain to civilization.

At the lower level of the mountain, on a well-used trail, I encountered another rider. I figured the stranger to be a cowboy, this part of the province being almost a desert with beautiful smelling pines, rattle snakes, and lots of cattle. Good guess. The conversation went along these lines.

"What are you doing here, round eyes?" asked my cowboy, who was obviously aboriginal.

"Prospecting," was my reply.

"Not so quick, white boy. This is an Indian reserve. We own the mineral rights. You need our permission to prospect on the reserve."

"Right you are," I said. (I did not call him Tonto, as was later alleged.) "However, I was up on the Crown-granted claims about fifteen miles west of here. The claims show up on the mine recorder's maps, and from the look of the work and their inclusion on the claim map, I conclude that they pre-date the establishment of the reserve."

"Okay," said the First Nations guy. "You can have your claims, but you can't trespass on the reserve. We don't want you disturbing our cattle. This is a working ranch."

"Wrong again," I retorted. "The Mineral Act says you have to allow right of way to the extent of a roadway not less than fourteen feet in width."

I now knew the derivation of the term "redskins." He was puffing and sort of standing up and sitting down in his stirrups. I concluded that further discourse would only cause him more discomfort and trotted away with my packhorse.

My employers decided to drill the molybdenum showing, so with great effort I managed to help a driller get a small drill and camp materiel onto the claims, while the local First Nations guys looked on with less than benign thoughts running through their heads. When we started to cut down some trees to make a camp and build a tripod for the drill, we got a visit from an irate band member to whom I had to show the appropriate section on the use of resources available in my now well-worn copy of the Mineral Act.

I had established a very pleasant campsite on a beautiful creek from which the driller was pumping water for drilling. Every couple of days either my helper or I would ride down to the town of Oliver and pick up whatever we needed, as well as the local papers. The drilling, however, was not producing consistent results. We would drill a couple of barren holes, followed by a bonanza, followed by more barren holes.

As July approached, my crew demanded that as patriotic Canadians they be given a week off over the holiday then known as Dominion Day, to pay homage to those two great Canadians, Labatt and Molson. They had been working ten-hour shifts, so I could see no harm in shutting things down for a week. We left our homey little campsite and headed for town. I made all the necessary arrangements at the ranch I was using for stabling my horse and renting horses for the crew. Sarah Richter, the proprietress, asked me what I had done about the camp.

"Hmm," she said.

"You don't think the Indians will bother it or steal any of the equipment, do you?" I asked.

"No," she replied. "It's probably okay."

I spent the holiday week in Kelowna with an old friend water-skiing and being as patriotic as my bladder would allow. I left a day early to get into camp ahead of the crew with supplies. As Headlight and I made our way up through the pines, the smell of Ponderosa had given way to that of cow droppings, which seemed much more plentiful than when I had left.

I found about fifty cattle in the camp. They had knocked down the tents, walked over the Coleman stove, broken the kerosene lamps, and defecated everywhere. The place was uninhabitable. Most of the cattle wandered away as I approached, but there was one tight-knit group standing in a circle with their heads down. They were not going to abandon whatever it was they were doing. When I pushed through their wall of backsides, I found the focus of their interest. There in the centre of my campsite was a great big white salt lick. Obviously my neighbours had deposited it there during my absence and nature had taken care of the rest.

That's not all. There were about a dozen cattle down at the creek, drinking copious amounts of water and occasionally emptying their bowels. The creek was now polluted. Once satiated with salt, the cattle would wander down to the creek for a nice cold drink of water.

Needless to say we had to move camp upstream and rebuild. As we were doing so, the original aboriginal who had confronted me rode in.

"Oh, there it is," he said. "I wondered where that lick got to. It must have fallen off the packhorse." He picked it up and rode off.

II

Flying with the WASPs

4

You've Got to Be Kidding

AROUND 1962 a tired old sulphur-producing company from the southern US began drilling a property near Timmins, Ontario. Bernard Baruch had incorporated Texas Gulf Sulphur in the 1920s to commercialize the Frasch sulphur process. It was a great success, but as the years moved on, competition increased from new sources of raw sulphur from other processes and sources. The tired old men of Texas Gulf, deciding to take a "flutter" because the sulphur business was going nowhere, tried to find a new metal-mining property that might revive the company's prospects.

The best place to look for a mine is while standing on the site of an existing one. At Timmins there were a number of the world's great gold mines, so where better to look?

I don't know if the lads were looking for gold when they drilled the Kidd Creek property near that city, but they found one hell of a copper/zinc mine. However, while they were drilling the ore body, they neglected to tell the shareholders or the public about the spectacular results they were getting. It was only after the field personnel and the directors had filled their hats with $17 shares that they announced to the world that they had found one of the world's largest and richest ore bodies.

Is that quote on the NYSE I see for the Texas Gulf shares at $58 correct? But only yesterday it was $17. The US Securities and Exchange Commission was highly un-amused. It was not going to condone the importation to America of the sleazy share-ramping practices of its northern neighbour. To the disgust of us all, they outlawed insider trading and their moves were promptly aped by the Canadian exchanges. This in spite of the fact that famous American fortunes, such as those built by the swashbuckling Fisk, Gould, and Kennedy, had been attained through the careful application of insider trading.

There were even stranger events at the time. A company called Windfall Mines had property adjacent to Texas Gulf's big find at Kidd Creek. Windfall was run by the successful and well-known mining promoter Viola MacMillan. While news of the spectacular results from the adjoining property was being released to the public, she was questioned about the results of the drilling program on Windfall's claims, to which she would say, "You are really going to be surprised." Unbeknownst to the speculators, Viola was driving around Toronto with the core from the Windfall drilling in the trunk of her car.

Calls were out for the Toronto Stock Exchange to suspend the shares until her surprising news could be disseminated. However, the suspension didn't come about for some time. A member of the board of the exchange, while walking his dog in the upscale neighbourhood of Rosedale, had encountered a package of unregistered Windfall shares that had just fallen out of a speeding car with a very low, sagging back end. Whether or not his good fortune influenced his decision to maintain trading of the Windfall shares remains a topic of debate to this day.

Finally, in late 1965, Viola announced the big surprise. Just how spectacular was the core in her car trunk? Surprise! It was a bust. The antics of Viola and the folks at Texas Gulf poisoned, stabbed, shot, and beat to death the golden, zinc, copper, and silver goose I was plucking. Viola got the Order of Canada. I got stuffed.

One of the reasons for my headlong rush to financial freedom at thirty-five was that I had difficulty working in the cold as a result of an industrial accident in Alaska. My challenge was to find a way to use my skills as a geologist while not working in the field in the winter.

Computers were coming into the mining industry right around this time, and my second major was mathematics. In 1966 Kennecott Copper hired me to apply computers to mining problems in their Salt Lake City, Utah, office. One of the constant problems confronting mine management was determining the viability of newfound deposits. Would they make money? If so, how would you measure the profitability? Computer models could provide the answer to those questions.

My credentials as a bon vivant at the school of nursing were tarnished, so I determined that I might as well get married, which I did. My career as an inside trader was finished and a life as a technocrat seemed a fitting end. As a last hurrah, I bought the Jag.

The years dragged by in Utah. The skiing was great, the beer watery, and no other jobs were on offer. Until a phone call in April 1969 from Toronto. Falconbridge Nickel Mines wanted me.

While in Utah I had pursued two objectives. One was the mastery of deep-powder skiing. The second was convincing my wife to accept Mormonism and hence polygamy. But only the skiing worked out. One out of two wasn't bad, but there was no upside. Better to leave.

It was wonderful. Falconbridge was in the computing Stone Age and the pace of bringing them out of it was electrifying. But then, just as the price of my remittance man friend's British pounds had fallen off a cliff, so did the price of nickel. A round of belt tightening was in order. I was out, along with the entire computer effort.

I was sitting in the now defunct basement cafeteria of the King Edward Hotel in Toronto when a headhunter approached me. Randy Wood (also now defunct) said that what I did for mining companies with computers could be done for the other side of the financial equation, the investors. Banks and brokers, he pointed out, had to know the profitability of various mining developments in order to discern which ones to provide either loan or equity financing. Randy got me hired as a mining analyst by the now defunct investment firm A.E. Ames & Co.

Little did I realize that my hiring was as much a political move as a technical one.

When I was introduced around the research department by the new director of research, I discovered that the venerable old firm already had a mining analyst. This struck me as odd until one of the old hands explained the terrain to me. The new director of research had found that his existing mining analyst did not have the industry background (he was an oil geologist) or presentability needed for the position. But the head of research department had a problem. Firing the current mining analyst would be a slap in the face to the previous director of research, showing bad judgment on his part. The news was less than thrilling: I had been hired to squeeze the current mining analyst out.

After having been given my first assignment, to determine the outlook for Inco (which meant write a buy report so Ames could participate in the next financing), I collected the data I needed and asked my secretary where the computer data–entry staff were located. There were none. The horrible thought of having to do my own keypunching ran through my head. Where was the computing centre? We didn't have one. How would I do my calculations? With the mechanical Friden calculator on my desk.

Luckily I had kept copies of my old computer programs from my Kennnecott and Falconbridge days. That weekend I went into the IBM computing centre and began modifying the programs to work from the investor's point of view and knowledge base. During my days in the office I would collect the information I needed. After work I would go to the computing centre to do the analysis. While in my office I would continuously punch the Friden so sounds of hand calculation emanated from my office. The biggest chore was transcribing the clearly printed computer output to illegible handcrafted spreadsheets for presentation to my boss.

Needless to say, he was amazed by the volume of work I was accomplishing. I didn't tell him my dirty little secret about having moved into the computer age while my colleagues were still punching calculators. I pitied my predecessor. My boss was sure to be waving reams of spreadsheets at him, showing what a real analyst could do.

My analysis of Inco showed that in the year 1972, at $50 a share, the stock was a sell. This was unheard of. Brokers never issued sell recommendations, because they would lose the underwriting ties with the target company. I was given more variables. I spent more evenings with IBM. My sell recommendation became even better defined the more information I was given. Inco was a Wood Gundy or Dominion Securities corporate-finance client that seldom, if ever, did any business, so the Ames sell recommendation was published.

It became a great bestseller because there were few, if any, investors who had ever seen a sell recommendation of any sort. People who didn't even own the shares called Ames and asked for a copy just to be able to revel in a sell recommendation. For a while I thought the report was going to be bronzed and placed over the office doors. The efficient market theory prevailed, and within six months the shares were on sale at $25 each. No, they had not been split. Only the price had been halved.

Ames, like all WASP investment firms, the only kind around at the time, was populated by the ne'er-do-well male offspring of the gentry. If Chauncey couldn't make it as a doctor, then law school would have to do. Well, maybe law school was asking a little much; let's think in terms of accountancy. At the mention of bean counting, however, both Chauncey and the senior male member of the clan would harrumph in unison and calls would be made to old friends in the investment business. So when the Inco sell recommendation by the BDG (or big dumb Greek) turned into a winner, questions were asked as to how this could have happened. Wasn't someone at Ames tipped off by an Inco insider that things weren't that good in the nickel business? Were the firm's lines of communication breaking down? Where were our friends when we needed them?

Then came the recriminations. Many of the firm's salespeople had heard that the sell recommendation was based on pure research rather than a tip from someone inside Inco and therefore hadn't acted on the advice. Their clients had seen the value of their Inco holdings halved.

When I walked through the retail sales area I was regarded with a mixture of fear, respect, and loathing. Why hadn't I been more forceful? I should have rubber-hosed anyone who didn't sell their Inco shares when the price was still in the high $40 range.

The head of institutional stock sales took me aside and asked whom I knew at Inco and when had I been tipped off. Could we rely on my source in the future? I replied that there were certain salient points that he and the other Ames salespeople were missing. First, I had worked for Falconbridge, Inco's only real competitor, where I wasn't even allowed to say the name of the latter company without spitting afterwards and crossing myself. Second, the reason I was working at Ames was that I had been laid off as a result of a crash in the nickel market. When I showed up in the Ames office as a laid-off support staff from Falconbridge, it should not have taken immense reasoning power to figure out that things weren't going well at Falconbridge and that this implied that all companies in the nickel business would soon see their profits plunge.

Okay, that's lateral thinking, something that's pretty difficult to do when you have spent your whole life thinking vertically, as in pecking orders.

So the chinless wonders concluded that I was lucky, which was better for them than my being smart.

My next undertaking with my secret computing centre was Denison Mines. I announced at the research meeting that I had concluded there was a uranium shortage developing and would be writing a buy story on Denison. You could hear head gaskets blowing out all the way down to the corner office. Did I not realize that Denison was run by a man who was a DP from Czechoslovakia? A mining promoter? To make things worse, he was short and had a chin. The man prayed with some sort of Eastern Christianity movement and couldn't get accepted at Lyford Quay.

Great. Lyford Quay. The place was developed by E.P. Taylor, a man who had made a fortune through insider trading when Ontario legalized beer bars. Taylor was a trader in brewery shares. In the 1930s, two days before the province of Ontario's announcement that it would be loosening its liquor laws, he bought up all the shares he could find in breweries, having received a tip from a person of quality in the government. Now compared with Stephen B. Roman, *there* was a man of quality. Mind you, I had a soft spot for Taylor, based on my old modus operandi.

How did Roman and the Denison empire evolve? It started with Joe Hirshhorn, a mining promoter who had come up to Canada from the US during the gold boom occasioned by the US Mint's raising of the price of gold in the 1930s. Hirshhorn had middling success in Canada until he financed Franc Joubin. The latter was beyond brilliant. He found gold mines in British Columbia, not to mention mines in Africa and Eastern Canada. Joubin made so much money that he gave his daughter a French count for a husband. Call me if you can top that.

It was the 1950s and the only country in the world to ever use atomic bombs on civilian populations had decided that it needed even more uranium for its peaceful pursuits. The US Atomic Energy Commission was desperately seeking the uranium for somewhat peaceful purposes before the Russians could mass produce atomic bombs. They would give a mining contract to anyone who could show a promising deposit, and that contract was something you could take to the bank.

Hirshhorn had been told by Joubin that there was an almost circular structure at Blind River, Ontario, with showings of uranium. It was similar to something he had seen in Africa, and that had become a real producer, he said. The two men arranged for the staking of the circular structure and started developing mines on the showings. You may well be wondering what lay at the centre of all this uranium at the rim of what appeared to be a saucer. Right. More uranium.

The centre claims were acquired by Roman, an oil and mining promoter. He put the best holdings into a shell company he had in his stable named Denison and started drilling. When Hirshhorn determined that Denison was having some success and that Roman need more money, he went to the latter's office and offered to buy from the treasury a million shares at $2. Roman had asked $2.50 a share. The conversation was reported as follows.

"Mr. Roman, that is my final offer: $2 a share."

"Mr. Hirshhorn, I can't take less than $2.25."

"Mr. Roman, you are a horse's ass."

Roman, as I mentioned, was a Slovak. His reply was, "In my country, Mr. Hirshhorn, that is considered a compliment."

Roman went down the street to the Doherty Roadhouse & McQuaig brokerage, which gave him $2.25 a share for the million shares. And so Hirshhorn lost the opportunity to control all of the largest uranium-producing area in Canada, and Roman became a multi-millionaire.

It was now 1972 and a burst of nuclear power–plant building was going on as a result of a presumed glut of uranium. US Atomic Energy Commission contracts were ending. Everyone therefore assumed that there was plenty to go around. In fact, one of the reasons to build power plants was precisely the glut of these contracts. The US government had enrichment plants for bomb manufacturing that were lying idle after having cost billions of dollars to build. The plants could become useful again if the world adopted the high-pressure water nuclear reactor developed by the US government, which was on offer to the world at bargain-basement prices from Westinghouse and General Electric.

What no one had thought of was that the there was a three-year cycle from the time the uranium entered the US government's enrichment plants until it emerged as fuel at the other end. So you had to take three years of consumption out of the available supply. Uh oh. There actually was a shortage. I proved it with one of my commodity computer programs and an IBM 360 computer at the computing centre, translating my findings into the usual handwritten spreadsheets.

My uranium report came out in 1972, with Denison as the top pick, followed by Rio Algom Mining, the operator of the mines on the Elliot Lake basin rim. Ames took the share price of Denison from $17 to $49. The Europeans couldn't get enough of it. As I rode down the street on my bicycle (you may ask what happened to the Jag, but more on that later), people would point and say, "There goes the uranium man."

When a firm becomes the "box" on a stock, it is gift from the avarice gods. Your traders know who bought the stock, who the sellers are, and where to place any shares that become available. So if you wanted a hundred thousand shares of Denison, whom did you call? The venerable firm of A.E. Ames. I was being sent around the world to flog the report and portfolio managers would scribble down every utterance I made.

I was given copious amounts of money and shares in Ames. The share deal was terrific. Ames would offer you their stock at a price dependent on book value (assets minus liabilities). Let's say that is $35 a share. The Royal Bank would lend you $31.50 a share to buy it at prime plus a half. That is how secure the brokerage business was in Canada. It was a cartel with fixed rates and limited entry availability, though that was changing. Even in those golden years the banks actually owned the brokerage firms. They put up all the money, because the principals could find better use for their capital, and none of their other assets, as loan collateral could command such low interest rates.

I knew a partnership was not too far off in the future. I could see my name emblazoned on the firm's letterhead. "Alexander C. Doulis, B.Sc., C.F.A." would be next to all those WASP-sounding names like Harris, Andrews, Mathews, Bellamy, et al. It was all too thrilling.

I was busy analysing the markets for aluminum, copper, zinc, and uranium. How the hell could I follow the gold market – not that it mattered, because the US Mint fixed the price. I didn't stop to think that the US was involved in a costly war in Vietnam and that as far back as Aristophanes in 421 BC the world has known that wars are paid for by debasing the currency. As the great Greek playwright stated in his production *The Frogs* during the Peloponnesian War:

> *Where is the silver Drachma of old?*
> *Or the recent gold coins?*
> *So clear stamped and worth their weight,*
> *Through the known world have ceased to circulate.*

Now Athenians shoppers go to market,
With their pockets full of shoddy silver-plated coppers.

The Americans had chosen to pay for their war by printing dollars. The more they printed, the less gold and silver there was to back them. Nixon closed the US Mint's gold window in August 1970. You could no longer exchange a US dollar for one thirty-fifth of an ounce of gold, nor could you exchange your US $5 bill for four ounces of silver.

The firm decided I needed a helper to do the legwork on the gold companies, so I hired Bob Buchan. Yup, the same one who went on to establish Kinross Gold. Not only did Bob pick up the rudiments of mining finance at Ames, but he even found his wife, the lovely Tina, on the sales floor. But Bob was not the only one to pass through the graduate school of finance that Ames had become. There were others who actually changed the course of the investment business in Canada. One such was the smartest man in the world, Peter Hyland, who was leaving Ames as I entered. But you were wondering about my Jag.

5

Jaguar Is Dead, Long Live Raleigh

WHEN I moved to Toronto, I bought a house in Cabbagetown that had previously housed three welfare families. Having been built in 1884, it had a mews in the back for horses (which had been redeveloped for housing) and no garage. So I parked in front of my house on the little dead-end street (excuse me, cul-de-sac) on which I lived.

Now, Cabbagetown is a downtown Toronto neighbourhood that over the years has become gentrified. Its greatest benefit is that it is an easy walk from the towers of finance. So I seldom used my Jag. One morning as I left the house I saw a yellow piece of paper on its windshield. It was a summons for having improperly parked my car. It seems that there is a law in Toronto for parking for "an inordinate period of time" in the early-morning hours.

When I got to my office I called the local police division.

"Good morning. I have a ticket for parking for 'an inordinate period of time' on my street. What's that all about?"

"Where do you live?" said one of Toronto's finest.

"I live on a cul-de-sac off the St. James Cemetery."

"Oh yeah, one of the dead-end streets. Know it well. You were parked overnight, which is a violation of the city's bylaws."

"What is the reason for the bylaw?" I asked.

"We have to control the flow of traffic, and illegally parked cars interfere with traffic flow."

I could just picture the residents of the cemetery hopping up at the crack of dawn to head for their day jobs and there was my car, impeding their progress.

"That doesn't make sense," I said. "As you admitted, I live on a dead-end street running into a cemetery. There is unlikely to be any traffic at all, never mind during the nights."

"Well, even on those cul-de-sacs you might have to get an emergency vehicle like a fire engine or ambulance up the street," the constable replied.

"I doubt that the presence of a piece of yellow paper on my windshield will speed the passage of an emergency vehicle down my street."

The constable's patience had worn thin, very thin. "Look, we don't make the laws. City council does. We enforce them. If you have a complaint, call your alderman. Goodbye."

Still smarting from a stale doughnut, I thought. There had to be more rational minds about.

At the time two left-wing firebrands, John Sewell and Karl Jaffray, represented my area of Toronto. I reached Jaffray and went through all the above arguments.

Karl was adamant. "We have to stop this overnight parking scourge," he said.

I am as opposed to scourges as the next guy, so I wanted to join city hall's campaign. "Great," I said. "I'll join that movement. I notice that the tickets are only issued once every three weeks. If we are going to put an end to this stain on the city's honour, we'll have to move to ticketing every night. I'll call the local police division and ask them to enforce the law every night in our neighbourhood."

"You can't do that," Karl said. "The citizens will be beating down the doors of city hall. I will rescind any such request on your part."

"Karl, it is beginning to appear to me that the city is using the traffic laws as a source of income. I don't think that is at all virtuous. In fact, that smells. I am going to destroy that system."

"First off, you can't," he said. "And secondly, never tear down anything unless you have something to replace it with."

Very prophetic words. But also a dare.

Now I am not allowed to lie in any filing or reporting I do with exchanges and commissions, but all levels of government find the truth hard to deal with. It is an orphan that no government will consider for paternity. I found this overnight parking fine a hypocritical lie, a particularly galling one because it only hit people without garages and those were, primarily, the poor living in the older parts of town. Always tax the poor; they can afford it: they have no cottages or yachts to pay for.

The heinous crime of overnight parking could be absolved by the payment of $2 by cheque to the city. Quick and easy. No fuss, just send in the money. I concluded that they weren't playing fair and that there was no need for me to conduct myself in a gentlemanly fashion. I wrote a cheque out for $2.05 to cover the fine, had it certified, and mailed it in.

A week later I found the cheque had been returned to me as being for the incorrect amount. I sent the cheque back with a note indicating that the cheque covered the amount of the fine and was better than a plain personal cheque because it was certified. I also indicated that if city hall was unable to accept good payment, then I would keep the cheque and consider the debt paid in full.

They accepted it and subsequent cheques for more than the amount of the fine. I now had the walls of the core shack off. It was just about time to do the logging.

After the passage of about six months, I phoned city hall and pointed out that they owed me fifty-five cents from overnight parking. The nice young man was adamant. I owed them money, he said. They couldn't possibly owe me money. I insisted he look up the records.

"You're right. We owe you fifty-five cents. I can't imagine how this happened."

I wasn't about to enlighten him. "Could I have my money back?" I asked. "A cheque will suffice."

There was an audible gulp on the other end. I knew as any bureaucrat did that a cheque to issue and reconcile would cost over three bucks. Not a great way to make money for the city. So my young man called for a seasoned street fighter to represent the city. After an inordinate period of time their champion came on the phone.

"You're right, Doulis. We owe you fifty-five cents. Come down to city hall and pick it up."

A good thrust but hardly a body blow. My opponent knew that I would have to wait half an hour, minimum, to get to the counter at old city hall to collect my money. His counterattack just grazed me and set me up for my killer punch.

"Look, seeing as you admit I have a credit, my next cheque may be for less than the required $2. If it is, please just debit my account. Oh, and if you find a note signed by me authorizing a charge to my account for one of my neighbours who may be a little short of the monthly parking fee, just debit that amount from the account."

City hall's shares were in a tailspin. The grief in my opponent's voice was obvious. "Mr. Doulis" – note that I now was entitled to some respect – "the city is not in the business of keeping books for the citizenry." (An exact quote.)

"You've already taken on the chore, now live with it," I said. "Ta, ta. Have a nice day."

It gets worse. I wrote up my little tantrum in the neighbourhood news-paper, *Ward Seven News*. All over the area you could see people lining up at their local banks and having their cheques for some amount over $2 and payable to city hall certified.

It was a disaster for the bureaucrats. The books had to balance. The appearance of some unallocated funds caused heads to turn and noses to sniff. Was that strange amount a political payoff? An allocation for the alderman's girlfriend? Maybe it's where next year's election funding was coming from. Phone calls were made. Some of the more seasoned chaps at Ames took me aside and opined that maybe I had been working too hard and that if I took a deep breath I would see the futility of this sort of thing, so ungentlemanly.

The city wasn't about to give up a million-dollar business without a battle. Karl Jaffray's prophetic words came into play. The city had a fall-back position. Not quite as lucrative and probably harder to institute, but it could be done. Although the citizens had paid through their taxes to have the streets in front of their houses paved, the city was now going to rent this space out to them. That's a hard sell, but they did it. The residents of downtown could purchase a monthly pass that would allow them to park on the street overnight and thus legally impede the flow of traffic and those all-important emergency vehicles going up dead-end streets. It was not a new or unique idea. It had been formulated in the Middle Ages by one of the popes and was termed an indulgence. If you wanted to kill your busi-ness partner in those days you just bought a dispensation from the Pope and ran him through with your sword or poisoned him at lunch.

I couldn't see myself being extorted by the city, so the Jag (a beautiful 1959 XK 150) was sold and a Raleigh three-speed purchased. For twenty years I never got a ticket of any kind. Many a night I would roll home by cab or limo from the oasis of Bay Street completely in my cups and end up safe in my bed with no fears of drunk driving or anything similar. My greatest danger after a night of martini gulping was that someone would step on my knuckles as I made it from the curb to my doorstep. Everybody was better off.

My employers, however, were less than amused. My stay at Ames and its very existence were soon to end.

6

The Old-fashioned Ways

W HAT was A.E. Ames? Who was Alfred Ernest Ames? He was a poor
bank clerk from Lambeth, Ontario, who came to Toronto and established
what became the largest underwriter of corporate and government securities in Canada and did it the old-fashioned way, a Canadian variation of
the Horatio Alger story. He married the boss's daughter. So what is really
important is, who was the boss?

That was Senator George A. Cox, whom I first encountered on page
274 of *A History of Canadian Wealth* by Gustavus Myers. Cox had been an
insurance agent. When in 1870 the Midland Railway Company of Canada
went into bankruptcy, Cox managed to get control for $0.22 on the dollar
and sold it to the Grand Trunk at about ten times what he paid for it. Then,
as a millionaire, he established the Imperial Life Insurance Company and
controlled upward of forty Canadian companies, including the Canadian
Bank of Commerce, the *Globe and Mail* newspaper, Canada Permanent
Trust, and Canada Life Assurance, to mention a few.

In 1899 his daughter married the impoverished bank clerk Alfred Ernest
Ames. The senator wasn't about to foist his new son-in-law on one of the
existing investment firms, nor was he to be allowed to continue clerking at
the Royal Bank. His daughter married to a stock salesman? A bank clerk?
No way. So the senator gave the young man a nice shiny new investment
firm complete with a list of underwriting clients (the forty companies he
controlled plus those of his cronies) and called it A.E. Ames & Co.

When in 1929 the new Canada Permanent Trust Company building
opened on the corner of Bay and Adelaide Streets in Toronto, the first three

floors were built to accommodate the Ames firm. To this day you can still see the private elevator just to the left of the main door on Bay Street. It only went up three floors. The Ames name is still discernible on the lintel over the door. They don't make fathers-in-law like that anymore.

Alfred Ames died in 1934, but the firm was so well entrenched that its momentum kept it rolling along. After all, when you are the underwriter for half the provinces in Canada as well as Alcan, Bell, and Hydro-Québec – you get the picture – it's hard to fail. To boot, the company had a large portion of the Government of Canada bond syndicate. Government bonds – there's another crop that never fails.

Fortunately, after World War II the hostilities between the Montreal and Toronto offices of Ames came to an end. Fred Chapman took control in Montreal, and while competition was increasing from all sides, he managed to keep Ames number one in Canada. Mind you he didn't do much for keeping Canada at peace. One evening, around 7 p.m., a French Canadian janitor rolled his bucket and mop onto an elevator occupied by Chapman and the latter put his foot on the bucket and shot it out the door. On another occasion, he arrived late in Montreal by train from New York after having sold an entire Bell bond issue and stopped in at the Queen Elizabeth Hotel dining room for a wonderful steak. He asked the French Canadian waiter what would go well with this bloody piece of meat.

"Rosé," was the answer.

"Excuse me?"

"Rosé, monsieur."

At which point Chapman leapt up, overturning the table and yelling for the maitre d' to immediately fire the poor unsuspecting waiter.

And you thought René Lévêsque fought for Quebec separatism.

But Chapman was nothing if not unrelenting in his campaign to put those damnable French Canadians in their place. Ames convened a meeting to announce a new Hydro-Québec bond issue with an interest rate that was beyond too high, just this side of usury, thus guaranteeing that the syndicate would have no difficulty in offloading the issue. He was approached by a dapper young man who asked, in a French-tinged accent, if perhaps the interest rate assigned to the bonds was not a tad high.

"Get out of my way, you worm," was Chapman's reply to the future premier of Quebec, Jacques Parizeau.

Chapman's death, in 1968, left the firm in limbo. There was a rule barring nepotism in brokerage operations. This was a problem because the remaining partners and directors of the company had been so dwarfed by the figure of Chapman, no clear successor could be found and a series of compromises ensued.

But then, in 1973, a miracle occurred. The aforementioned Lévêsque, a pure-wool French Canadian separatist, almost got elected premier of Quebec. Montreal, which had been the financial capital of Canada, saw all its wealth transferred overnight to Toronto. Armoured cars carried securities and financial records down the Trans Canada Highway for days. The price of real estate in Toronto revived for the first time in years, and all the clubs had their waiting lists doubled as the WASPs of Montreal buzzed en masse to Toronto.

Ames Toronto was now supreme. To make things worse, the Montreal office now had French-sounding names on the roster. The underwriting clients had moved to Toronto, as had much of the wealth management of Canada. It was the total defeat of Ames Montreal.

As for me, things were going swimmingly. Except for one minor irritant. Although I was given plenty of perks, such as club memberships, a director's expense account, and travel, I was still not a partner or director, even though I owned more than enough stock to qualify. After the uranium study, the headhunters started coming around in droves. I was, in the parlance of the street, "A Big Swinging Dick."

The frenzy for my services was increased because none of the other firms even had a uranium analyst. I served as a "learned witness" at a US court hearing into the takeover of Stanrock Uranium by Denison Mines. Chuck Parmalee, a director and finance guy at Denison, took *me* to lunch. There was always the invitation to the Denison annual meeting and Christmas party – both extremely lavish events still unsurpassed in Canadian corporate life.

I went to the then president of Ames, a former retail sales guy. "Peter, I've been approached by a number of firms on the street," I said

"Nonsense."

He was right. I hadn't been approached by the actual firms but by headhunters representing those firms. It clearly stipulated in the Toronto Stock Exchange rules that poaching within the local game preserve that was the

Toronto brokerage community was forbidden. As a result, an industry of talent scouts had sprouted up, making the pitch on behalf of the firm that wasn't poaching.

"Well, let's say that there is a position for me as a director at Doherty Roadhouse."

"Pshaw. A bucket shop. No clients of quality. Bloody wire house. Completely unsuitable."

By wire house my mentor meant that the firm took orders from its own and other small firms across Canada and executed them on the floor of the exchange, a rather lucrative business.

"As well," I said, "I've been told that Peter Hyland at A.E. Osler is keen to have me over there and that I could negotiate letterhead status."

"Osler, fine firm. I know Dick Lauber well. Warned him not to let that Hyland gang in the door and now they run the firm. Hyland and that crowd of his will never make it in this business. We only gave him a job here because of his father. Good Montreal family. Alcan, if memory serves."

It was typical of people at Ames to refer to an individual by his under-writing ties to the firm. If you said Scrivener, someone would say Bell. If you said Crump, they said Canadian Pacific. Also, the events at A.E. Osler were to presage the changes coming in the industry. But it was being made abundantly clear to me that I should turn a deaf ear to all overtures. Were I to leave the Ames fold I would sooner or later end up in bucket-shop hell or selling unlisted garbage securities through a broker-dealer. Having had my negotiating position reduced to drivel, I finally popped the question.

"Well, then, how about a directorship or something?"

"Unsatisfied? Can't give you much more money. That would distort the remuneration scales. How about a director's expense account and Stanley Cup tickets? Tell you what, I'll even throw in a summer vacation to your old homeland, Italy."

This confused me greatly. I was of Greek descent. But then maybe Peter was a history scholar and knew that the Greeks, prior to the birth of Christ, had colonized most of Italy. I was losing the thread of this conversation. So I went back to basics. Christmas was fast approaching and it would be nice to take something home. Within the brokerage community, festive gener-osity knew no bounds. "Just a directorship or partnership – something simple and enduring – would be nice," I said.

"Can't be done, lad. The letterhead."

I thought I understood the problem. If the firm made me a partner or director, then all the stationery would have to be changed. Only the envelopes could be saved. But I had an answer for this. "Don't put it on the letterhead until we use up all the old print stock," I said.

"You don't understand," our president said. "We can't have an ethnic name on the letterhead. What would the clients think? But there is a way around that. Mathews changed his name from some Polish thing like Milewski. Nobody knows he's Polish. You can do the same. Doulis could be changed to Donald, or Davis. Something proper sounding."

"That wouldn't be such a good idea," I said. "I am known as Doulis the uranium man. Clients want to hear from Doulis. What are we going to do when Manufacturers Life calls and says, 'I want to talk to Doulis'? Are we going to have the switchboard say that they are transferring the call to Davis née Doulis? And anyway, Dominion Securities has Dombroski on their letterhead. You can't get more ethnic than that."

"Yes, but Jim's family has been around for a long time. He's a member of all the clubs. It's not the same."

"Peter, I can save everybody a lot of trouble. I'll just change my name to Dombroski."

He appeared stunned by my flexibility. "Good idea," he said. "As for the name-recognition thing, I'll have to speak to the board about that."

I left shaking my head, wondering if "Dombroski" was moving up or down the ethnicity scales.

7

The Death of Scrooge

CHRISTMAS came and any sighting of Scrooge on Bay Street brought out the heavy guns of gift-giving. In fact, Christmas was a year-round affair in the financial world. But that was brought about by a highly remunerative business in an oligopoly. The product was identical: the transaction of the sale or purchase of shares at a fixed price. Competition had to be on a different plane, and it was based on service and generosity.

The institutional stock business differs from the retail business in the size of orders. Something like the municipal employees pension fund doesn't trade in five hundred–share blocks. For them to have a meaningful representation in an investment, they need hundreds of thousands of shares. If the pension fund were to ask a dealer to purchase that number on the floor of the exchange, the price of the issue would skyrocket. To avoid that, the dealer will try to find existing blocks of shares in the ten to one-hundred thousands share size and buy those.

Also, the institutional investor is not interested in hot tips. He is not going to buy Dry Gulch Gold Mines for his fund until the company has a proven reserve. The fund manager wants research. He wants to believe, when he buys a stock, that he has been told all there is to know about the company.

Because commissions were fixed, this was a very lucrative business. A hundred-thousand share purchase could net $10,000 in commission. If the broker did both the buy and sell, it was worth $20,000.

It was also a very competitive business. Commissions were fixed by the exchange, so other ways had to be found to compete. One of those was the quality of research on the fundamentals of a company. On the research side, the efficient-market thesis said that all that could be known about a company was priced into the shares. The analyst had to look for something unknown to the street. That was tough, but the quality of analysis was improving as the upstart firms were getting into the business. Where the upstarts could not compete was in the old-boy connections and the three B's: broads, booze, and billets (French for tickets).

For example, while in France on a sales trip I went out for dinner with the Ames Paris representative. After dinner he had the limousine stop by a swank block of flats near the opera where we waited until a man from the Newfoundland Department of Finance exited one of the buildings doing up his fly. I doubt that he had gone there to relieve himself.

On the booze side, any celebratory occasion, such as weddings, funerals, or bar mitzvahs, was a good reason to send the client a case of Margaux, Chambertin, or Dom. I once heard of a case of bubbly being sent along to celebrate the birth of a portfolio manager's child by his mistress. I remarked to the sales staff that I thought this largesse should be limited to legitimate children. The wives could get jealous for receiving only still wines.

So Christmas was the time of great gift-giving. But what do you give the man who has everything? In my geologist days they would say ten thousand units of penicillin. In my brokerage days they substituted dollars. You are right. You can't just walk up and give Laird Laidback $10,000, so you use the Hillary Trade. This is named after the smartest commodities trader in the world, the wife of Bill Clinton of Oval Office fame. What makes her so brilliant is that, starting in October 1978 and ending in July 1979, in an account over which only she had trading authority, she made $100,000 with seldom, if ever, having initiated a trade on her own. She was smart enough to never venture into the trading pits again. The matter would not have come to light if she hadn't forgotten to include the gain in her income for taxation purposes.

How is this done?? The trade is set up thus. Someone in a trading firm puts through a contract for the client to buy a position in a commodity, say pork bellies. The price is struck at the opening of the market. If the price is increasing when the desired amount is achieved, the commodity is sold and the profit recorded to the client account. If the price begins to fall during the day, the position is covered and a short position established, which will be closed out at the required profit level. The client doesn't put up a dime and walks away with ten grand. In a cruder method, the time stamps on the tickets are set so as to assure a profit. To cover the unreal trades, a frenzy of buying and selling may occur, with no net effect on the account.

The stockbrokers wishing to remunerate a special client a pension or mutual fund used a variation. The client's personal account would have a position bought for him in a seldom-traded bond for which the broker did all the trading. The position would be closed out at the end of the day in that the firm would buy back the bonds from the client, but at a higher price. Voilà, a profit.

But gifts were also bestowed in other ways.

A skeleton staff had to be kept on during the Christmas holidays to take care of the parking. Parking was the movement out of a pension fund or other investment-management entity of securities that didn't look good. If you didn't want to be seen owning liquor or tobacco stocks in your life-insurance company's portfolio for year-end assessment by the trustees, you called your friendly broker and arranged the price at which you would sell before year-end and buy back the shares after year end. Suppose you took a flutter on Clairtone, Peter Munk's old company, and it was now on the ropes. You believe the government's going to bail them out and you want to own it when it happens. Best not to have it in the portfolio at year-end for your trustees to see.

And then there was the bond bull market at year-end when the brokers would post new, higher prices for the clients' inventory in order to assure the portfolio manager's bonus. After New Year's those higher prices wouldn't be seen again until the following Christmas. Ah the season of brotherly love.

What about the billets? Ames kept centre-ice season's tickets for both the Montreal and Toronto hockey teams. As well, they had as their Toronto doorman and elevator operator a Maple Leaf stadium usher. In New York they were much more cultured, so the tickets were front row for Broadway shows.

But the times they were a-changing.

As I was joining Ames, Peter Hyland was leaving to team up with Roy Birckett and Gordon Ewart to form the nucleus of an institutional operation. What they had was two analysts and a salesman. What they did not have was clearing or trading. To provide the latter, they struck a deal with an old, established retail broker, A.E. Osler. The only real competition they had, and it was tough, was Loewen Ondaatje McCutcheon. That firm had all three elements: trading, sales, and analysis.

Regardless of the competition, Hyland and his cohorts were doomed to unbridled success. What the institutional investors wanted, however, was an unbiased source of information rather then the standard feed from the old-line full-service investment firms where the mantra was, "We own therefore we recommend the purchase of ..." How could you get an honest research opinion on Nortel from the firm that was going to do the next underwriting or be part of the syndicate that sold the issue? Remember the $10,000 commission on an institutional trade? It didn't take many of those to make Hyland and his gang very wealthy, seeing that they had to be split only three ways.

But now gift-giving went the other way. I went to see the head of portfolio management at Canada Permanent Trust in the midst of a bear market when commissions had dried up and asked why we were getting such minuscule business from his desk. He informed me that he had to feed enough commission dollars to the independents to ensure their survival. So while the president of Ames was looking down his nose at the upstarts and competitors, I knew they were in a privileged position. And they didn't have to live on the three B's principle, which could get expensive.

The one outpost where the upstarts had yet to penetrate in the mid-1970s was Europe. Institutions had a lust for North American shares, for two reasons. One was that there were industries such as mining and utilities that were unavailable on their exchanges. The other was that the corporations listed on the European bourses were a crapshoot. The accounting was meaningless, insider trading was rampant, and shareholder rights non-existent. For that reason there were hardly any retail-share markets in Europe; the small investors preferred bonds where the ability to abuse the investor was minimized. For the European capitalist, shares were an interest-free loan from the public.

I arrived at the Ames Paris office as the BSD and was introduced to our man in Paris, Count Amadeus de Pompiginon. His first words to me were: "Don't call me Amede. Call me Monsieur." My reply, obviously, was, as loud as possible, "Sure, whatever, Amede." This was the distinguished gentleman who waited for a Deputy Minister of Finance to get his zipper up after a tryst with a tart. In less refined quarters that is called pimping. I was told by the drillers I consorted with during my geologist days that the only time to call a pimp sir was when he was holding a knife or some other weapon. I was obviously in uncharted waters here in Europe.

Amede had arranged a lunch at his club, which I thought was a coronation. As I stood at the receiving line for the gentlemen entering, I was introduced to a gaggle of counts, barons, marquises, and pretenders to some title or other. My thoughts raced back to the French Revolution. Hadn't Robespierre beheaded all of the French nobility? Maybe they were similar to some of the lower forms of life like crabs that re-grow amputated body parts. What did impress me and leaves me wondering to this day was the depth of their understanding of North America. Not just the facts but the subterranean things that made it tick. So, as well as understanding their country and continent, they were fully versed on mine.

The next stop on my itinerary was Lausanne, Switzerland, home of Ames in the land of the gnomes. This was another eye-opener. When our man Jean Claude Blanc and his office colleagues took to me to dinner at one of their homes, I couldn't help but ask what kind of neighbourhood we were in.

"Niarchos of shipping fame lives next door. Why do you ask?"

"It's just that I haven't seen many homeowners with a submachine gun in their front closet."

My host explained that every able-bodied man in Switzerland had to be in the militia, which was the country's main line of defence. Everybody had their weapons at home in case of a call-up. Virtually every home contained a gun or two, yet the country had virtually no gun crime. I guess they hadn't heard of gun registries, the one sure way to get weapons into the hands of criminals. I was fascinated also by the idea of where the artillery people kept their weapons, but didn't get a chance to ask. We had to discuss the gnomes rather than guns.

When the French Revolution broke out, the wealthy of that country moved their assets to Switzerland under the requirement that no information be given out to the revolutionary authorities who were pursuing this wealth. So it was that bank secrecy arose. Then the clients demanded that the Swiss bankers invest their funds. The Swiss thought about the prospect of inside work with no heavy lifting and decided this was the profession for them.

The Swiss developed some of the tactics used to this day for separating the investor from his money. First, when you left your funds with the Swiss banker, he had to charge you a management fee. Somebody had to pay for the expertise necessary to manage your money. Once you paid that, the manager of your assets would now buy in-house funds, which had a management fee built in as well.

When a Swiss private banker bought a block of shares for its clients, it would, on foreign issues, act as principal. In other words, they bought for their account and then sold to their clients at a markup. If the client decided to sell, the sale would be made to the "house" at a discount from market and then the "house" would sell the shares in the market for its account at a slightly higher price. Needless to say, it was difficult for the clients to get rich from the actions of their money managers, but this kind of money was most often looking for security, not significant growth. If the portfolio manager matched inflation, the client was re-signed.

Much of this money was in flight. The largest portion had been squirreled out of some high-tax country and now resided in a numbered account. The owner of the account was probably someone for whom even a small investment income would be soundly thrashed by the tax collectors. Other money, such a Marc Rich's, had been acquired by circumventing US trade embargoes and taxes. Although as an American citizen Rich was required to pay tax on the money he made violating US laws, he preferred not to. Marc's money didn't have to earn much; it just had to stay outside the US.

So it was with much of the money sloshing around in Swiss banks. Business was booming.

The 1970s saw a number of tinpot dictatorships around the world established by the US to keep the world free. There is a distinct lack of job security working as a US-backed tyrant. Think of the shah of Iran, Noriega of Panama, or Marcos of the Philippines. No pension, no health plans. You had better look after yourself for that rainy day when you would be de-elected. Most incumbent dictators therefore kept their own and as much of their country's wealth as they could get their hands on in Swiss banks. There was always the possibility that your tenure could be terminated by your sponsors or those ungrateful wretches, your countrymen, for whom you toiled as much as possible between more important duties on the French Riviera.

As for the Marcoses of Philippines fame, through some accounting mix-up, $300 million of the state's money got confused with theirs. Not being mathematically inclined, the family couldn't sort it out. It took almost the threat of war to get the Swiss to give up any of it.

The Swiss, however, were great clients for us. The constant inflow of funds and the growth of funds from interest earned meant that they were always buyers. One of the local wags confirmed to me that he had seen share certificates in their vaults so old they were written on clay tablets. The other great thing about dealing with them was you didn't have to bribe the fund managers. You had to bribe their employers, the bank. This meant sending them client business, commission breaks, and deep discounts on bonds. They also demanded disproportionate pieces of new issues. Everybody worked for the house and there was no fishing allowed off the company pier. It made life much simpler than in Canada where you never knew if the bribe, excuse me, gift you were giving was going to the right person. Could the recipient of your largesse actually direct business to your trading desk? In Canada the company pier was so crowded, lines got tangled and people fell off. One such event happened to me.

8

Coal in the Christmas Stocking

AMES had underwritten the Kaiser coal operation in B.C. It was a roaring success and everyone made a bundle. The Japanese steel industry was expanding and there was good-grade coking coal in the province just looking for a blast furnace near Yokohama.

The Japanese had a yen for it. After the underwriting, I was given the responsibility of following the company's future. Pretty dull stuff, because the basis of the business was fixed-price contracts and volumes. However, there were not any other publicly traded coal companies in Canada, so I was accepted as the man to call if you had a question about coal.

And a question did arise.

One day a voice on the other end of the phone asked if I knew where to buy coal.

I said I could find supply if the volumes weren't great and the quality specifications not too severe. "I know the market pretty well and I haven't heard of any shortfalls," I said.

"This isn't a shortfall per se. It is a created shortfall."

"Who are you and who do you represent?"

"When will you next be in Montreal?"

This was getting weird. Coal wasn't traded out of Montreal. My caller had a French accent and call display had yet to be invented. I was talking to a Gallic deep throat.

"I'm supposed to be there in two weeks."

"Have dinner with me on Tuesday at eight at Chez George on Mountain Street. Speak to George and tell him your name."

This was beyond understanding. I thought of Ames Montreal clients. Could it have been Pierre Lassonde from Beutel Goodman? He and Ned Goodman were looking for greener fields than just money management. Aside from the analyst at the Caisse de dépôt (the Quebec version of Canada Pension Plan), he was the only one I knew in the financial arena who was French Canadian. I figured it must be some kind of joke. I didn't mind, because I was fond of Chez George, which always served an excellent steak tartare and had a superb Saint-Julien in its cellar. Whoever my contact was, he knew something of my preferences in Montreal.

My introduction to Chez George had been at the hands of Pierre Gauthier, a salesman at Ames who was about thirty with salt and pepper hair and Gallic good looks that reduced women to simpering oafs. He took me to the restaurant without a reservation; it seemed to be a mark of recognition to be seated when all about you were standing. While George struggled to find Pierre a table, a young lady approached us at the bar. She was gorgeous. She strode up to my host and the conversation went thus:

"Pierre, you haven't called."

"But Denise, you were to call me."

"Merde. You're right. I remember now. I lost the scrap of paper with your number."

"No problem. I'll be sure that won't happen again. Denise, are you wearing pantyhose or your usual garter belt?"

Before I knew what was happening, Denise had exposed her thigh between the top of her stockings and her undergarments and Pierre had scribbled his number there. I thought back on the event and concluded that I would most likely be meeting Pierre at Chez George. He was always able to surprise.

But as with many assumptions, this one proved to be wrong.

On the appointed Tuesday, I went to the local stockbroker/client bar at the Queen Elizabeth Hotel and quaffed a few until 7:30 and then walked over to Chez George. I climbed the stairs and looked around for Pierre, but he hadn't arrived. I asked for a martini and stopped George as he came by.

"Have you seen Pierre?"

"Non, monsieur."

"Perhaps he has a reservation for tonight?"

"Ah, Monsieur Alex. I remember. Your host is already seated. Let me take you."

As we wandered through the restaurant, I looked for a familiar face, to no avail. We approached a table and a late middle–aged man stood up.

"Alex, I am Jacques. Please sit down."

"My pleasure. Have we met before?"

"No, but I've heard much about you. Let's order. I understand you are fond of Saint-Julien and I've asked for a good year to be opened."

I'd only been an analyst for four years but recognized the value and intent of good research. My host was telling me he was serious enough to check me out and that he might know a lot about me. It was like going into a corporate-finance meeting to propose a new issue or takeover. You had to catch the listener's interest right at the start and if possible put him a little off balance. It had worked. I was a little nervous.

After dinner Jacques called George over with the cigar box. I took a Monte Cristo, while Jacques settled on a nice-looking Romeo e Julieta.

"To what do I owe this fine evening?" I asked.

I was hoping you, as Canada's preeminent authority on coal, would be able to buy some coal for a friend of mine. He wants no less than twenty thousand tonnes or more than eighty thousand at a time. Can you find those quantities?"

"Possibly, but there are the factors of quality and price to consider," I said. "Top-grade coking coal is hard to find, though at times it shows up in Appalachia and B.C. as production overruns. What kind of specifications are you looking for? Low ash, low sulphur?"

"Just the opposite. My client wants high ash and sulphur is irrelevant. Moisture content will be limited."

"What you are looking for is coal that is not destined for the steel industry. I can't think of a blast furnace that will take high ash or sulphur. Where is the coal going?"

My host rolled his cigar between his thumb and forefinger and stared at it intently. He was trying to figure out how much he could tell me and how much he needed to.

"The coal will be going to cement kilns."

"Where?" I asked.

"Europe."

"Where in Europe?"

"Spain, Belgium, and Italy."

"Jacques, this is like pulling teeth. Can you tell me the whole story? I think I can get what you want, but it's a question of quantities and shipping, mostly. Just tell me what you want to do as a complete undertaking and we can work together. Coal doesn't deserve all this mystery."

"A friend of mine has a contract to supply coal to the European cement cartel." he said.

This was fabulous news. This cartel had a government-recognized, controlled market throughout Europe. Prices were fixed and any increase in costs passed on directly to the customers, which to a great extent were governments. Okay, so retirement at thirty-five was gone, but my new buddy was opening the door to getting out at forty. The golden goose had been revived, though it had turned coal black.

"How much, how often, and for how long?" I asked.

"I don't know. It depends on the pricing."

"Jacques, this should be a very simple undertaking. We determine the monthly volumes and act as broker. We buy the coal and mark it up to an FOB* price and cash our cheques. What's the problem?"

"My associates told me to go into the details if absolutely necessary and it appears I have no choice. My friend is a former senior bureaucrat in the Quebec government who took early retirement in the face of a scandal involving the province and some major banking interest in Europe. He was not really involved but chose to fall on his sword to maintain the integrity of all involved and bring the affair to a quick, quiet end."

This was starting to make some sense, because the banks in Europe controlled the companies that controlled the cement industry. "So where does the coal come in?" I asked.

"The coal is going to be used as a way to recompense my principal for the loss of prestige and pension he has incurred for the benefit of his colleagues. The cartel is willing to buy coal from my associate at whatever price, within reason, to provide him with a satisfactory reward. He needs now only to find the coal."

---

*FOB means Free on Board: the seller pays the cost of transportation to the port of shipment.

"How much coal and for how long?"

"We don't know. It depends on the spreads between what is bought and what is sold. The objective is to get a predetermined amount of funds into my principal's hands."

I thought about it. This was another variation on the Hillary trade. Did I want to get involved? What were the ethical considerations versus my position as an analyst at a brokerage firm? If this should make the headlines, would I take a hit? Could I possibly get a short-term contract without serious volume commitments?

"Jacques, this is fraught with difficulties," I said. "No one is going to give me a contract that is open-ended. Therefore I can't guarantee price. Also, I don't know what my position is with respect to my firm. Nor do I know the legality of all this."

"I assure you, mon ami, that this has been thought out by better minds than ours, and as a lawyer I can find no possible liabilities. With regard to price, everything will be done on a spot basis. You will need no contracts."

"What's in this for me? What kind of a commission am I looking at?"

"There is no commission. You are being paid a guarantee fee."

"But I'm not guaranteeing anything," I said. "I don't want that kind of liability."

"Your guarantee will be that the material on the dock is coal as defined in the geological sense."

"That seems bizarre. Why would I do that?"

"Guarantees are not defined in the Canadian tax act. So you won't be liable for tax on any of the payments you receive from the cartel. The people putting up the money are not interested in having to pay you and your income tax as well, so they have found a tax-efficient way to pay you. They want to minimize their costs. They are therefore doing everything in the most tax-efficient manner."

"When this money hits my bank account, questions are going to be asked," I said.

"The money will not be going into your account. There will be a corporate account in Zurich from which only you will be able to withdraw money, and the amount will be determined by the amount of coal delivered."

"Jacques, what you're asking me to do is find coal for which you will pay me a finder's fee. That's all. I just have to tell you where it is and you do the rest. Am I right?"

"Almost, Alex. You have to be more careful how you define your remuneration. You are not receiving a finder's fee, you are receiving a guarantee fee."

"How do I tell you that I have located some coal? You'll have to give me your card."

"I left the hotel so quickly I neglected to bring some with me. But you can contact me through this gentleman in Paris."

He handed me a card of a man who was an "advocat" on the Boulevard Haussmann. Another damned lawyer.

"Jacques, I have to admit this whole thing sounds weird to me. Are you a principal in this deal?"

"No. I've been hired to speak to you."

"I'll have to think about it."

"Dear boy, you've been asked to find coal and you will be paid fifty cents a tonne in a Zurich bank for every tonne that is taken. You have no liability and no risk. This, as you say in your business, is a buy or sell decision. There is no hold. Take it or leave it, now."

"Okay, but under two conditions. I get paid sixty cents a tonne, and you tell me how much money we have to get to your principal."

"Sixty cents is fine and we are trying to accommodate a million dollars."

We parted and I went to the Chateau Champlain and thought about what had just happened. I had accepted because if my research showed that this was too risky, I could just "not find" any coal. I also called the restaurant and spoke to George.

"I lost the card of that man I had dinner with tonight. Who is he and what is the correct spelling of his name? Do you have his phone number?"

"Monsieur Alex, I have never seen the man before. From the telephone number he left with his reservation, I'd say he was staying at the Queen Elizabeth Hotel."

I couldn't very well phone the Queen E and ask for Jacques. I took the deal. I sent my passport to the Paris lawyer and got it back a month later, accompanied by a pass book from Credit Suisse's Zurich office. This was my first introduction to the offshore, but I didn't pay much attention at the time because I was making big bucks and tax rates back then were still in reasonable territory.

What did catch my attention was how many times and in how many ways financial markets were used to funnel money to people. I figured that it would take a two dollar per–tonne premium on five hundred thousand tonnes of coal to get the "principal" paid off his million bucks. I stood to make $30,000, paid into a Zurich account.

Life could not have been better.

9

It Wasn't Meant to Be Non-profit

TIMES were a-changing. Rapidman had come out with a hand-held calculator and the Commodore 64 computer was hitting the shelves. It now looked like everybody would be going electronic for financial analysis. My advantage was about to be lost. And there was other troubling news. It was 1975 and I had a bucket of Ames shares but still had not changed my name to Dombroski. I did not have the privilege of attending the board meetings where all was revealed, but I did get to attend the annual meetings where the financial statements were flashed onto a screen and then everyone got drunk. There was no hard copy to take away with you.

There were now a number of analysts as shareholders. Sue Scully, Joe Leinwand, and Tom Starkey were among the august group owning shares. We were all miffed that we couldn't sit down with the statements to see what was going on. All we saw was the slide on the screen of each page of the statements and then a drinks tray. Some of my colleagues conspired to act with me to record the more important of the pages of the statements as they were flashed. Each person was responsible for a portion of a different page. I had liabilities from the balance sheet as my responsibility. I am surprised that management had not conceived of the idea that the analysts would find a way to get the numbers. That was what Ames paid them to do for listed and unlisted corporations. Get the real numbers. You couldn't be an analyst if you didn't have numbers to analyse.

The Monday following the annual meeting the crumpled, booze-stained pages were put together to give a good picture of what was happening at Ames. For me what was of concern was that contingency accounts were being run down to provide non-operating earnings and continue to pay the dividends necessary to cover the interest on all of our shareholdings. The bond desk was having trouble maintaining its profits as competition increased.

As well, costs were going through the roof. Looking at my expense account and those of others who out-spent me two to one, it was clear why. I knew of directors spending $2,500 a month at Winston's Restaurant. Why not? They owned a portion of it. It was said that when John Arena left the Rosedale Golf Club, some of the members who objected to the way he was treated financed a restaurant venture for him in downtown Toronto's banking district. These were the same golfers who practiced their putting in the directors' offices of A.E. Ames & Co. and lunched as often as possible at Winston's.

Then there were the foreign offices, such as the swanky Ames House in St. James in London and the "two balconies" on the Place Vendome in Paris for the count. Tokyo had also been added as a high-cost non-profit centre. As an analyst I could see that there was not a strong management team in place to correct this.

There were rumours that this would change. I decided to wait another year. You couldn't sell your shares without leaving the firm. What with all my perks and great remuneration, I didn't want to leave, but I was worried about continuing to own the shares. All those concerns would eventually be revealed as trivial compared with what really happened.

10

Where the Ginza Never Sleeps

I was sent to Japan by Ames in late 1975. Except for an unpleasant incident, I enjoyed it immensely. So much so that I intend to take my second wife there soon. Oh, the first wife. The one with the aversion to Mormonism. I thought you'd never ask.

While in Tokyo I was working like a sled dog during a gold rush by day and drinking ersatz Scotch whisky with the salarymen like a sailor on his first night in port by night. My body was taking a beating because there was a desire on the part of every one of them to drink the guijin (foreigners) under the table as revenge for the war in the Pacific. Our man in Tokyo, Colin Ross, finally insisted I go to the Tokyo Onsen, the big downtown bathhouse.

"Colin, I don't need a bath," I said. "I need rest."

"This isn't a bath as you know it," he replied.

"I am not going to one of those sleazy massage parlours, if that's what you had in mind. I'm a married man with a child."

"Alex, this is a traditional Japanese bathhouse, all very above board. Believe me, you need this."

I took the card Colin gave me and grabbed a cab. As I walked in a kid by the door said, "Shine, Misser?" I didn't even reply. I was going to get this done and be back in time to entertain Yamaichi Securities, that night's vengeance seekers. I paid the equivalent of $10 to the lady at the wicket, and she motioned for me to sit on a bench. My Japanese was passable so I got by that part. Within minutes another Japanese lady came up and grabbed me by the sleeve. She hustled me down a hallway and into a smallish room. In the corner there was a small bathtub with hot water overflowing onto the floor and into a drain.

"In there," she said to me in Japanese.

She was pointing to what looked to be a closet but turned out to be a sauna. I took off my clothes and thought, what a wonderful idea, a sauna. I needed that. In about five minutes I heard an egg timer ring, and the lady came and opened the door on my now naked body. She pointed to a stone table in the centre of the room and placed a step for me to ascend. I was obviously meant to lie on the slab.

Here comes the sleazy part, I thought. So I lay face down. The lady dipped a wooden bucket in the steaming, overflowing bathtub and threw its contents over me. At first I figured this was another one of those revenge things. This time it was for being a smart ass and lying face down. When I tried to roll over, the scalding buckets kept coming. I decided to protect what I cherished most and held my position. The drain was gurgling as my dominatrix put down her bucket, stubbed out her cigarette, and started with a scrubbing brush on my body. I couldn't tell if this was heaven or hell but was tending toward the former, even though my puritanical instincts warned me off.

The woman was scouring my buttocks when all of sudden she let out a shriek and jumped back. "Tak san guijin," she screamed. What she had said was, "Very large foreigner."

I thought about the comment and wondered how she knew when I was face down. Then it struck me: it was my entire body she was referring to. Then another revelation: the woman was blind. All my prudishness had been a waste; the profession of the masseuse in the bathhouse is reserved for the blind. After she regained her composure, she laid into me with the brush and renewed gusto. I wondered if thoughts of Midway, the Battle of the Coral Sea, Okinawa, and Iwo Jima were running through her twisted mind, but enjoyed it anyway.

I was really starting to recover when the woman screamed, "Guijin," and pointed to the tub in the corner. It was the old lobster trick. But as I lowered myself in the water, it felt not unpleasant. I had become acclimatized to the temperature from her constant sloshing of water over me. The egg timer chimed again and I was directed back to the slab. I was ordered to roll over onto my stomach whereupon the woman jumped on my back and placed her bony knees below my rib cage and worked her way down my back to the sounds of a Rice Krispies commercial with snapping, crack-ing, and popping. It was fabulous. Then, when she put her thumbs deep into my shoulders and I was contemplating the heavens, her egg timer sounded and she was gone.

I put on my clothes and looked at the fresh new me. God, I was going to tear out the livers of those guys from Yamaichi with goblets of Suntory Scotch. Remember Pearl Harbor? It was payback time. Let's see how many doubles it takes to separate the men from the salarymen. As I was walking out, the same shoeshine boy said, "Shine, misser?"

"Hit it kid. Make the wingtips sparkle. We're on a mission tonight." None of which made any sense to him, but when I put my shoe on the stand and flipped him a hundred yen, we reached an understanding.

So, it became a routine. My schedule consisted of making the rounds with Colin Ross, heading off to the bathhouse at day's end, going back to the hotel to grab a fresh shirt and cigar, and then bring the real investment message to the natives. I was starting to settle in to Nippon Lite as a way of life. My linguistic skills were improving to the extent that I was becom-ing quite arrogant. I actually knew the word that every Japanese refuses to say: "No." It is an affront to refuse someone something in the Japanese culture. To have heard the word "Eya" put you a cut above the run-of-the-mill round eyes.

Then things started to unravel. We were out for dinner with Nomura Securities and had finished a passable French meal while sitting cross-legged in a restaurant attached to a geisha house. My host said, "Something else, Doulis-san?"

I turned to the waiter lingering nearby and said, "Sumasen, hanake codesai." Which meant, as far as I was concerned, "Pardon me, but I want a cigar." He looked at me in a state of confusion, so I applied the method I use with French Canadians who pretend not to understand my French: I said it louder and more forcefully. I fully expected the dolt to run out and bring the cigar box. Instead, he stood as if transfixed. The restaurant had gone dead silent. You could have heard a chopstick drop.

I knew something had gone wrong, so I turned to my host, who said, "Doulis-san, you want a cigar?"

"That is what I have precisely asked this oaf to bring. Doesn't anyone here understand Japanese?"

Japanese etiquette barred my host from pointing out an error on my part, so an instruction was in order.

"Doulis-san, you have asked for hanake, while actually wanting a hamake."

"Same thing," I snorted.

"Not quite. 'Hana' means 'hair' and 'ke' means nose. You actually asked for nasal hair."

He then saved the day by very gruffly demanding the cigar box as if it had been the waiter's mistake.

The evening was long, but worse was to come. After much bowing I got into a cab and headed for the Imperial Hotel. I thought I'd give Barbara, my wife, a call and inform her that I would indeed make it home for Christmas, which was about a week away. It was late enough in Tokyo to be morning in Toronto.

I asked the desk to connect me to my home number. When Barbara answered the phone, I said, "Barbara – great news. I am going to be home for Christmas."

"Don't put yourself out. I'll be divorcing you when you get back," was her response.

I slammed the phone on the table and yelled, "Who is this? What number is this?" Goddamned Japanese could never understand English. So they screwed this up. Happens all the time. They just can't understand numbers.

What seemed to be Barbara's voice now used the English Canadian-speaking French format but talked slowly as well.

"Thank you for sharing that with me," I said. "Good night."

I couldn't very well go out and get drunk because I already was. I couldn't go to the bathhouse because I had just been there four hours ago. I fell asleep in my clothes and awoke in the morning to the usual call from the desk. I figured I'd work things out when I got home. Get everything back on track. I'd been spending much too much time on the road recently. I'd have to kick back a bit. Save the old marriage.

11

Killer PMS

I was not overly surprised to find no one waiting for me at the Toronto airport. I was dog-tired and there were no bathhouses or blind masseurs in Toronto. In fact, in 1975, there was only one sushi bar. The whole Ginza thing seemed to have been a booze-induced dream. The only joy was on the part of my liver, which was really happy to have left Japan.

The next day was Christmas Eve. We were to spend it with our best friends, Gary and Marly. Gary brought his bike and he and I went for a ride up the trail that paralleled one of Toronto's major traffic arteries, the Don Valley Parkway. Yes, that's right. On December 24, 1975, it was warm enough to cycle. Of course we were the only ones on the trail so we rode side by side.

"Barbara says she is going to leave me," I told him.

"Yeah. I heard. Things are really weird. Here we are cycling in December, your sister-in-law has come out of the closet and left her husband for another woman, and your wife wants to leave you for her career."

"What are you talking about? What career?"

"Well, I guess she figures if a big dumb Greek can become a Big Swinging Dick, she can, too."

I was pretty sure this would prove anatomically difficult for my wife. But I could see what had happened. She had become bored. My son, Christos, and I took our vacations without her so she could get a break from mothering. We would spend a week at the cottage alone smoking cigars (his second hand) and peeing into the lake with no female guidance to impose civility on our lives. Then on weekends we would go to kids' theatre and wander around the shops and cafés eating what we shouldn't while Mom recharged her batteries. It was patently obvious. Divorce on the grounds of infidelity. I had left my wife for my son. It was apparent I'd have a tough time patching this up.

I was right. She left New Year's Day, taking my son with her. I was devastated. As local BSD, there was nothing I could do. Or could I?

When I got to the office I told the people that had to know about the marital situation and got down to work. There was what looked like a tree trunk of fax paper on my desk and a collection of phone-call slips that could have been recycled into a Yellow Pages phone book.

The big problem was that my Swiss coal–company buddies had lost twenty thousand tonnes of coal. A ship had called at Point Roberts, B.C., to pick up the shipment, only to find the pier empty. Nobody at the port could find the coal.

Well I wouldn't think so. It was in Prince Rupert, B.C., somewhat farther north. So let's look for the coal in Prince Roberts or was that Point Rupert or Prince Rupert? There are only four words and if you get two of them in the right sequence you find the coal. They had not read the invoice properly and assumed that a port name starting with "P" would be Point Roberts not Prince Rupert. The coal business was starting to wind down, presumably because we were getting close to the amount destined for my unknown partner in Quebec. I figured the guys in Brussels weren't going to pay him any more than agreed, so one of the forthcoming twenty thousand–tonne shipments would be the last. I had spoken to their man in Paris about continuing the business, who had said it would be a good idea if we cut out the Quebec partner. The Parisian's logic was that the guy no longer contributed anything, such as a final market.

"What will you contribute?" I asked.

"The billing, shipping, and banking."

"Where do we get the capital to finance the shipments?"

"If you haven't withdrawn any of your Zurich money, we can use that."

"What about your money?" I asked.

"Ah, monsieur. C'est fini. All gone."

As the smoke began wafting out of my ears and my head gasket was reaching dangerous pressures, I calmly said, "Ah, my friend, no pay, no play."

"What do you mean?" he asked.

"Pas d'argent, pas de jouer," I translated, dropping the phone into its cradle.

There were people around who would try any kind of nonsense believing that the counter party who had somehow amassed a significant amount of money was stupid enough to put it into their hands, even though all they were offering was an idea.

The next largest collection of phone slips consisted of calls from partners and lower-level directors from as far away as Vancouver. On most of them was the cryptic question, "Is it true?"

I walked out to the reception area and asked Carol what the secret message was.

She told me there was a rumour that Steve Roman, mining promoter, displaced person, non-Anglican (but probably Christian) Slovak and horse trader, was to have lunch in the Ames boardroom. I told Carol to phone all the yellow slips back and tell them that it was true and that it was a result of my efforts. They could therefore either damn me if they wanted to preserve the firm's untarnished WASP credentials or praise me if they wanted to keep making money. (A sedan chair with nubile maidens throwing rose petals in my way would suffice.)

You are right if you think my life was hitting a low point between divorce, sniping from the cheap seats, and a goofy French lawyer. But as my restaurateur grandfather used to say, what you lose on the steak, you make up on the hamburger.

At the end of the week I was absolutely ground down. I was the hamburger. I finished on Friday and went over to the Savarin Bar where most of the Ames folk went after work. I slumped at the bar and ordered a martini – three to one Tanqueray gin to one vermouth, lemon twist. I had just put rim to lip when that lovely girl from the executive offices sat down beside me at the bar. Being still in the age of tattered chivalry, I bought her a drink. There was a somewhat suggestive tone in her conversation, and I noticed that her skirt seemed shorter than when I saw her in the office that morning. Her legs now appeared to go all the way to her shoulders. I was still in shock from the week's events and said that I would soon be going home as I had a big day of shopping and cooking scheduled for tomorrow, Saturday. Dull stuff, I said. Better done alone. She left.

I turned back to the bar only to discover another sweet young thing sitting on the other side of me. Something to do with accounting or book-keeping or was it contracts? In any case I managed to convince her as well of the inappropriateness of the current circumstances. I looked in the mirror of the bar and saw that behind me was an unusually large presence of young ladies from Ames. I went to the washroom and took off my jacket. No, no one had painted a bull's-eye on my back. It was obvious that the Ames in-house wire service was at work.

There was another factor at work here. In the old days the WASPs would send their daughters to private schools where they could mingle with other girls of their status and hopefully not catch lesbianism. Having survived that, it was off to the University of Toronto to meet the chinless doctor, lawyer, whatever who would provide a fine hearth and a brood of new chinless wonders. But what was one to do with little Prudence, Martha, or Penelope who couldn't get into university? Or what about Mildred who screwed up her university career by getting straight A's, an honours B. Sc., and an M. Sc. and no "Mrs."? Marriage to a bank clerk? Not quite. Calls were made to the legal and brokerage firms as well as nursing schools. Things had to be set right. For God's sake, the girl was a complete failure: twenty-two with a master's degree in geophysics and no marriage prospects.

A young lady sent off to the farm leagues of matrimony knew that further screw-ups would lead to spinsterhood. The young ladies in the office of the professions had blood in their eyes and desperation in their veins. Not only was there competition from the sisterhood of friends and family daughters, but there also were those damned interlopers, the daughters of underwriting clients. Although poaching someone else's husband may have been somewhat accepted, the economics were as poor as the optics. If the first wife didn't move on, the newly acquired, slightly used husband had a significant and irreparable financial leak: alimony. It also took a few years until invitations would be forthcoming once again. This because the new divorcée was more than a little bitter, having seen all her work at bagging the big producer swept away in a flurry of low-cut bodices and high-cut skirts. The ex-wife would fight a battle of attrition, hoping to heap the greatest amount of social discomfort possible due to a man so unacceptable as to have left her. Or to have married her in the first place, for that matter.

And there I was, cast into the shark tank of matrimony.

The sharks in this tank were perfectly coiffed and manicured. Usually the ethnics like me were left for the lower ranks of the predators. Ethnics were considered like a Chinese meal. Half a decade later and you were still poor. But then there were the Big Swinging Dicks. These guys had established themselves and were fearless. They were beyond both lawyers and doctors. Any effort to land one of the BSDs was fair. Even if it was someone else's BSD. In my case I was a free-standing BSD. Even better. Also because the wife had left me, instead of the large financial leakage there would be just a drip.

This was the era of no HIV and the only dangerous kind of sex was that which a woman's husband learned about. I won't bore you with the seamy details, but within two months I was hiding out at the all-male Toronto racquet clubs with a strict directive to the bar steward that any calls for me from the female species were to be answered with, "He's just left, ma'am." One lady had her brother call on her behalf.

I had other things on my mind. The custody thing was dragging on and the Ames annual meeting was coming up. This was the drop-dead year for me. If there were no improvements in the firm's financial picture, I was going to have to sell my shares, which meant I'd have to resign.

My son, who was five at the time, was expressing dissatisfaction with his living arrangements. I had never consented to his mother having custody, but she had been well coached during my absence in Tokyo and knew that once she had walked out the door with my son she could keep him. My lawyer, Jim MacDonald, told me that I would get custody the day I learned to menstruate and that child-rearing had been deemed by the courts to be the realm of the sisterhood of tossed-off wives. My research suggested that a full fifteen percent of fathers actually ended up with custody, this in an era of gender equality. Gender inequality was like insider trading: nobody admitted to it but it was still rampant.

My love life had changed. I had taken myself out of the clutches of the soap opera "Desperate Husband Seekers." Living near me was a nurse married to a doctor. We would, on occasion, enjoy the sauna in her house in the late afternoons. On one such occasion she made some very cogent remarks.

"Alex, have you noticed anything about that parade of girls I see coming and going from your place?"

"Yeah. Leggy or cute."

"As well," she said, 'they are all papier-mâché mock-ups of your first wife."

"Good point. So what?"

"If it didn't work out with that kind of woman in the first instance, what makes you think that it will work on the second try?"

"I see why you're not sweating," I said. "There's wisdom pouring out of every lovely pore. But what you say makes sense. Don't worry, I've given up sex and become a monk. I only copulate for therapeutic purposes now."

"That's not what I am getting at. I have the perfect woman for you."

At the outset I knew it was a big mistake. The lady I met had a real bosom, short but attractive legs, and not a drop of blood on her canine teeth. Being a gentleman, I decided to tough it out and at least have a pleasant dinner. She definitely was not my type, and although it has so far taken thirty years, I am sure I will be able to define what qualities are missing and point them out to her over breakfast one of these days.

My son was totally taken with the new mate and admitted to her that he wanted to live with his father. The lady was a child psychologist and said that it was normal for a child to say that to both separated parents. What I needed was a child psychologist or psychiatrist to interview the lad and trick his true feeling out of him. I liked the sounds of that, sort of like Perry Mason.

Somehow we ended up with a child psychiatrist whom I assessed as being so terrified of his own mother he felt that every mother had to be obeyed. After interviewing my son on a few instances and talking to each of his parents (but not scheduling interviews with their mates), he made his decision. As my son and I left his office on the way to the opera (Die Zauberflöte, great Mozart for kids), I told him he would be home soon. Two weeks later I had to break the news to him that the doctor had decided that what he really wanted (as did his internal mommy) was for Mom to have custody. Christos wasn't sad or disappointed. He was bloody angry.

"Look," I told him, "you should have made it perfectly clear to the doctor what your preferences were. I thought he was one of the subtle truth discerners, but he actually needs it spelled out."

"What do I do now?" he asked in desperation.

"You are the only one in control of your destiny. When you can say slowly and clearly to the doctor is that you want to live with me. Then he will figure out that you want to live with your father. He's good at deductive reasoning."

Six months later I still hadn't learned to menstruate, but my son had grown cajones. He wanted to speak to the doctor and wanted me present. I arranged the meeting.

"What did you want to see me about, Christos?" lisped the good doctor.

"I want to live with my father," Christos said, getting right to the point.

"What about your mother?"

"I don't think she wants to live with him."

"No, I mean what about her feelings? Maybe we can make the change over spring break."

These holidays were to occur in about two weeks. The doctor's strategy was that to save Mom (his subconscious one or my son's, I didn't know which) some heartache, Christos would come to stay over the holidays and not go back.

Christos's reply (he was now six) was, "How about tonight?"

I made sure the clever, insightful child psychiatrist had duly noted Christos's comments. In previous encounters with Christos, he had proven to be either deaf or lacking in note-taking skills. The following weekend he moved home (not the doctor, Christos). As a result of his being the child of divorce and experiencing the hardships, disappointments, and mental anguish of not living with Mom, I was unable to steer him away from a happy life and flourishing career in the investment industry.

Although at the time I didn't know that my son would end up working in my own field, I knew that I would end up in the poorhouse after the next Ames annual meeting if I didn't dump my Ames stock. I arranged my resignation and heard the audible sad sigh on the sales floor when it was announced that I would be leaving. No it wasn't the sales force sighing; it was the secretaries, who to that point were still holding out hope for a big score. I had arranged to move a half block west along Adelaide Street to the offices of Deacon Hodgson. It meant that I now had a half block more to cycle to work, and that instead of chaining my bike to a light pole I would be using a tree. This proved problematic.

12

BSD Meets LSD

IF you walk on the north side of Adelaide Street, between Bay and York streets, you will see in the background, while looking south, the great example of Bauhaus design, the TD Centre. In the foreground you will see a building with white marble, a sweeping rear entrance, and small windows. This is a classic of design known as Early Jewish Modern. Yes, First Canadian Place.

This design form needs trees. I was now working in the building that then existed to the west of it, the National Life Building. It had been built right to the property line and had no bike racks. First Canadian Place did have bike racks, but these were on its private property. I felt uneasy about using them, so I locked my bike to a tree planted in the sidewalk.

One day as I left to head home I found a piece of paper stuck to my bike, upon which was printed: "Your bicycle is parked on private property. Should you continue to do so, your chain will be cut and your bicycle removed at your cost and expense." It was signed PC 120.

I knew that Toronto policemen had four-digit numbers, so this was not a cop. I also knew that I was parked on the sidewalk, not on anyone's private property. When I arrived home I found one of those plastic tags that the airlines used to give you to identify your luggage. I typed on a card I cut to fit that envelope: "This bicycle is the property of Alex Doulis, 5 Laurier Ave., Toronto. Should you interfere or move this bicycle you will be charged with theft." I attached it to the Raleigh.

Around mid-April, while we were having dinner, a man arrived at our door in bib overalls, clutching a letter.

"You Doulis?"

"Yes."

"This is for you." He handed me the letter and walked off.

After dinner I opened the letter and found it was from Len Doohan, Assistant Commissioner of Public Works for the city of Toronto. I still have the letter somewhere but can remember it to this day.

> *Dear Sir:*
>
> *Complaint has been received and examination determined that your bicycle is parked on the sidewalk on Adelaide Street West causing an encumbrance on the public thoroughfare in violation of by-law 369-19.*
>
> *Should you continue to park in this manner you will be charged under the by-law.*
>
> > *Yours truly,*
> > *L. Doohan,*
> > *Assist. Com. Public Works*

I ignored this missive, figuring that even dim light bulbs burn out sooner or later. Things went well enough until the last week in April. I was heading over to my club, The Engineers, then located on the corner of Victoria and Richmond, for lunch. As I stepped out of the National Life Building I saw two men dancing around my bicycle waving a Polaroid camera. I went back to my desk and called the local papers. The two dudes were still there when I came out.

"Is this bicycle of interest to you?" I asked.

"Sure is."

"Well, you are in luck as it is mine. I see you're taking pictures. Why don't I cozy up to the bike, seeing as it's mine, so you can get a real good shot."

The shorter of the two, Doohan, was just bursting with glee at this suggestion. Greenway, his aide-de-camp, took the picture. As the photo slowly crept out of the camera, I noticed that the photographer had cut off the top of my head.

"This is appalling!" I shouted. "Look at what you've done. It's a perfectly simple chore. Take a picture of the entire scene. What good is this garbage? Waste of taxpayer money."

A passing policeman heard the shouting and inquired as to the cause of the disturbance. He, too, thought the picture a sad piece of work but agreed that Doohan had the right to demand the movement of my bicycle. By then a car from the *Toronto Sun* and one from the *Toronto Star* had arrived.

"Hey, Mr. Doohan, look, they've got a professional photographer," I said. "Let's all gather around the bike, including the police officer, and get a good shot. Something you can frame."

"I'm not going to be party to your soapboxing," Doohan said.

"Greenway, come on over. You'll look great."

Greenway was thick enough to start walking over to us, but Doohan ran up and caught him by the sleeve. So the constable and I smiled into the lens and when the photo op ended I demanded that Doohan and Greenway be given copies. The reporters crowded around and I gave them the story, complete with names and numbers.

That was April 24. On May 1 bicycle week began in the City of Toronto and there on the front page of the *Toronto Sun* was yours truly in his chalk-stripe, double-breasted suit, next to the little green Raleigh and the big bull cop. To make things worse, Dianne Francis wrote an article in the *Financial Post*, entitled "Cyclist Takes on Big Wheels." Bicycle week was not starting off as the city had planned.

A series of letters ensued. Mine I addressed to Roy Bremner, the Commissioner of Public Works, so he would know what his lads were working on. In his letters, Doohan informed that the trees were the property of the city. Although they stood smack in the middle of the sidewalk, they were not an encumbrance on the thoroughfare, but that anything attached to them would be on the sidewalk and hence be blocking the sidewalk.

Well, it was reasoning of a sort. I felt I could work with that. I went to city hall and looked at the site plan. It showed a number of benches on the sidewalk that were the property of Olympia and York, the company that owned First Canadian Place and was causing me all the trouble. In a letter I informed Doohan that these benches were not only an encumbrance but also a focal point for pickpockets, panhandlers, and women of low repute. They should be removed at once.

Doohan wrote back that the benches were not an encumbrance, with no reference to the abovementioned lowlifes.

Fine, I replied in a missive. From now on I would chain my bike on top of the benches, which are not impeding the sidewalk. No problem. As well,

Olympia and York could do nothing because the benches were on public property. Case closed.

Not quite.

While I was working on a report in my office at Deacon Hodgson, the corporate secretary knocked on my door and said there were two men from Olympia and York to see me. This struck him as odd because I was not a real-estate analyst.

"Put them in a client room. I'll take care of it," I said.

I was wearing a blue pinstripe suit with vest and gold watch and chain. I relit my cigar and walked in to meet the lads from O & Y. "Can I help you?" I asked.

"We're looking for Doulis."

"You're looking at him."

"Well, we expected a much younger man."

"I am forty years old, if that is any help."

"Look at that," said one of them. "He's forty and not a bit of grey hair."

I could not believe what I was hearing. Had they rehearsed this routine? Was there a script to follow or did you just provide the logical ad lib?

"Well, gentlemen," I said. "If you bicycled to work, as I do, you would look as youthful as I do." That was the right reply wasn't it? Was there a better line? I didn't think so. I let it lie there for a moment, waiting for the applause.

There was none. Just prolonged silence.

"How can I help you?" I asked.

"It's about your bicycle."

"Bicycle? I am in the middle of an important report and you want my bicycle? I am sure I don't understand."

"We're from O&Y and are here to bring an end to this problem with your bike."

"I have no problem with my bike. You do. You end *your* problem. You can do that by telling Len Doohan to take a hike. You started him. You turn him off. If your benches get scratched, blame Doohan. Just leave me alone."

"Okay, park your bike wherever you want."

"Thank you very much," I said. "It is so nice of O & Y to allow me to use the public thoroughfare in any manner I see fit. Good day, gentlemen."

I've never confirmed it but I was told that Len Doohan went from being

Assistant to the Public Works Commissioner to noise inspector in River-dale. This would seem logical, because Bremner was absolutely scrupulous and insisted that those about him not only be squeaky clean but appear so as well. He had received all the letters, and I'm sure he would not tolerate people in his department doing favours for commercial interests.

My position was clear. I could not allow the landlords to start dictating how the populace used the public space or it would never end. By this time I was a director of the Engineers Club and the Toronto Racquet Club, as well as being president of the Mineral Resource Analyst Group of Toronto. All my fellow officers and directors supported me. In one decade the obeisance to authority had disappeared.

13

God Stands Up for Bastards and Liberals

DEACON Hodgson was an interesting firm. As well as working diligently for the return of a Liberal provincial government, they ran a nice little brokerage business. It was profit focused and had some really great people. The ones that come to mind are Bob Acheson, or Ach as I called him, Rob Harris, and Major Barbara.

Ach knew all the usual accounts in the UK, but also those that nobody cared to service. Although they were obscure, some of them were of real size. We would walk into their offices, sometimes with the Major in tow. Her effect on the portfolio managers was electric. The Major stood a full six feet in her heels and had a peaches and cream complexion with the natural honey blond hair to match.

The poor simpering devils would open the conversation with, "What should I buy, how much, and at what price?" After that I would go into my routine about how Inco was now the stock to own because at a price of less than $30 and the prospects of climbing nickel usage in the stainless steel used for nuclear plants it was time to buy.

Ka-ching, thank you very much for your order.

It was beautiful time to be alive. After a day of ringing the cash register, the three of us would repair to somewhere like Bentley's on Swallow Street for a lobster bisque, Dover sole, and a couple of bottles of Montrachet.

Then the Americans found out about our secret weapon, the Major, and soon Lehman Brothers, Goldman Sachs, and Merrill Lynch were all showing off their new female stock salesmen to the Brits. I started to travel alone in the UK.

It was always an annoyance to go into some portfolio manager's office with an important presentation on a big company with a potential double and have the guy ask me about some penny dreadful.

"I say, Alex, have you heard about the Engineer Mine on Atlin Lake in Northern British Columbia? Apparently the mine produced a king's ransom in gold, which was on a boat that sank while crossing the lake. Everyone was lost, including the man who knew where the mine was."

"That's great, but I want to tell you about Inco. This stock is a double."

"Yes, yes, but you could make some real money here. I talk directly to the managing director and he tells me they are within a week or two of finding the big vein."

What do you do with this one? Tell him that you were laughing at this story the day Murray Pezim came along to ask you to log somebody else's core, and that was seventeen years ago? If you tell him the truth, he won't believe you and will kick you out of his office. When you come back a year later and the deal has collapsed, the client is going to say you, the analyst, should have known it was a fraud.

There was one unusual opportunity that was easier to get across because of technical problems that had yet to be solved. This one was a result of the fascinating geology of the Princeton area of British Columbia. There you have a relatively young layer of sedimentary rocks, some of which are coal beds. Through these a volcanic extrusion passed. What is coal? Carbon. What are diamonds? Carbon. While this hot magma had passed through the coal layers, it had picked up carbon in the form of coal and burned it, leaving a carbon residue, which, as a result of the heat and pressure from the magma, had turned into diamonds.

You may well wonder why you haven't heard much of the fabulous diamond fields of Princeton, though they were well promoted in Europe with the speculators being shown pieces of now frozen volcanic lava containing the minuscule gems. Nobody thought to ask how the miners were going to remove the brittle diamonds from the hard, solid rock containing them without ruining the gems. Diamonds are hard but also brittle. When you try to shatter the host, you shatter the gems. This same property under different corporate names was danced around Europe every ten or fifteen years and was sort of like an annuity for the promoters.

But it wasn't always a one-way street. I was given a pearl of wisdom that changed my outlook completely and shattered my faith. It started at the Confederation of British Industry, which represented British business interests in the same way the Chamber of Commerce does in Canada. Ach had found that it also had a very nice pension fund. At the time, the Hunt brothers of Texas had gained control of the silver market and run the price from $5 an ounce to $55. The professional traders had sold short. The only source of silver to cover their positions was available from the Hunts, but only at $55 an ounce. There was blood in the streets.

It was after lunch when I started my pitch to the CBI portfolio manager and when I did, he said, "Ah, commodities. Better get my man Martin." He picked up his phone and soon a short dumpy guy walked in with no jacket but wearing a vest upon which were distributed a variety of soup stains, not all from today's undertaking. After the introductions, Martin asked, "How do you think they'll do it?"

"Do what?"

"Change the rules for silver trading."

"The exchanges and the markets would never do that," I said. "It would be unethical. You can't change the rule in the middle of a game."

"Alex, what is the first objective of any institution?" Martin asked.

"Provide a service."

"No, that is the second objective. The first is self-preservation. Governments, religions, and even commodity exchanges look after their own destiny before satisfying the needs of their participants."

This soup-stained wonder proceeded to give me an example. "In 1923 a Frenchman managed to corner the market for copper on the London Metal Exchange. There were a number of traders representing member firms that had sold short to the Frenchman and when he demanded delivery there was no one to borrow or buy metal from except him. There were a number of haircuts about to be given not to mention some potential bankruptcies. There was only one answer, which was to change the rules.

"Until that time Chilean-produced copper had not been considered 'good delivery' against a sales contract on the London Metal Exchange. Now it was. So all those professional traders who found themselves short could now buy Chilean copper to fulfill their short positions and the marketplace could be saved. The Frenchman shot himself, and the National Bank of Paris, which had financed him, went broke and was reorganized."

"You're telling me the same is in store for silver?"

"Exactly, and the real shame is that there is no way to profit. If you sell short at this point you will be called for delivery after three days. You will know when the fix is in the day you see a huge wave of short selling. That will be the day the professionals have learned in advance that the rules have been changed."

My mind ran riot with remembrances of warrant short positions on the Vancouver Stock Exchange bringing grief to the members and the warrants suspended from trading until they expired worthless. Then there was Morty Shulman's cornering of a warrant position in Reichold Chemicals on the Toronto Stock Exchange. The professionals offered to deliver shares against the warrants they had sold short to Shulman. The courts ruled, however, that the shares were not the same security as the warrant and that they had to deliver to Mr. Shulman what they had sold him, warrants to buy shares, not the shares themselves. He became an overnight millionaire. There was only one response to Martin's insight.

"Martin, could you join me for dinner this evening?" I asked.

Although his boss coughed a lot, I did not invite him.

That evening, at the Savoy Grill, I watched as further claret stains were added to Martin's already multi-coloured vest. For that I was given more pearls of wisdom about institutions such as Greenpeace. As Martin explained it, Greenpeace was formed to end nuclear testing. When nuclear testing ended, did Greenpeace end? No, it discovered that gay, paraplegic, orphaned, single-parent whales were being slaughtered and rose to their defence. Which then leads me to ask, today, why are the laws against terrorism, which threaten the state, much more draconian than those against killers who threaten the individual? Why can you spend life in prison for buying ammonium nitrate fertilizer (a potential explosive), which may threaten the state, but only a few years for buying an illegal handgun and actually killing a citizen during a home invasion? You see, Martin had a very good point, didn't he?

On subsequent trips I tried to see Martin again, but his boss always declined further meetings, citing the press of business. I'm sure Martin went on to become a don at Oxbridge teaching something like Philosophical Economics. He may have even have bought a new vest.

I never called home from my semi-annual sales trip to Europe for fear of what might happen à la my call from Japan. Life had returned to a calm, measured pace. The Deacons were fun, the office convivial, and you got to meet a lot of out-of-work politicians. I continued to maintain my star ranking as an analyst and didn't have to scrounge around for coal for the cement kilns of Europe. It was serene, but all that was about to change. I was about to be introduced to the sheltered workshop of Canadian investing.

14

The Naughty and the Nice

THERE were tumultuous events taking place in the industry. Remember Peter Hyland and his merry band? They had become disgustingly rich and taken over A.E. Osler. To secure for themselves some penetration of the Montreal market, which still had a little life left in it, they bought the tired old firm of Wills Bickell. Old man Bickell had made a fortune out of the Timmins gold rush, having been a big promoter of the old McIntyre Mine. His house still stands in Mississauga and was at one time owned by the real-estate tycoon Bruce McLaughlin. Bickell's backyard is now the Mississauga Golf Course.

Upon Bickell's death, the firm struggled to stay alive and was seen by Hyland and cohorts as the door to more Montreal business. When they acquired Wills Bickell they also acquired Alistair Stevens. He quickly went to work alienating the three amigos, Hyland, Ewart, and Birckett, from each other. He almost had control of the firm for his efforts when Birckett and Ewart departed. Hyland was still holding out.

I'm told that at what appeared to be the top of the market, Peter Hyland, who happened to be my doubles partner at the Toronto Racquets Club, managed to get himself fired by confronting a senior partner at A.E. Osler about the marital status of his parents at the time of his birth and the extent of his manliness. What would you do? Fire the man. Which the partner did. Peter then reached in his pocket and produced the partnership agreement requiring the immediate buyout of a partner's position in the firm if dismissed. No waiting, no phased withdrawal, just immediate payout and game over.

In the pre-bank era, the ownership or equity of an investment firm traded at book value between the existing private shareholders. The liabilities were subtracted from the assets on the balance sheet and the remaining amount was due to the shareholders. When a shareholder left, it was traditional that he would get screwed a little along with his goodbye kiss. This was accomplished by marking down the value of the assets and increasing that of the liabilities. Voilà! We have a firm that is now worth fifteen percent less than the day before the departure. These values would be maintained until payout at month end or whenever.

The only exception was when someone was fired, at which time the books were frozen. Peter's move was considered at the time a masterstroke. You don't mess around with the smartest man in the world.

I had heard about Hyland's departure from A.E. Osler because it was a cause célèbre in our little community. I had not heard about where he had landed after Osler. Peter, or Ginger as he was called, for his copper-coloured hair, was a rather taciturn individual. Our conversations after a game consisted solely of market chatter.

For example, at around this time he asked me: "You having any fun over at Deacon?"

"Same old, same old," I replied. "Suspicious wives, poor speculations, not enough business. What about you?"

"I hooked up with Connacher over at Gordon Securities. It could prove to be interesting. A lot of bench strength for trading but short on everything else. I need some of 'else.' I'm the director of research, and I've got Ed Zederynko doing the oils and myself the steels. I need a ranked mining guy. You're ranked."

"What about Chris Thomson? I thought he did the mines over at your shop."

"He's not ranked, so he's moving on."

"I thought John Lloyd-Price did the oils for you guys. Isn't Zederynko more of a speculative stock guy?"

"Lloyd-Price is a deal guy. He's left over from the old days of Gordon Securities when Monty Gordon and Gordon Eberts set it up as a deal-making shop. He's kind of pissed at the way the Gordon shop missed the merger with Bell Guinlock. He's probably going to tie up with Eberts and Monty Gordon. We need some trades on the blotter. People listen to

Zederynko. He moves stocks. You can move stocks. Also, we've been pushing some stuff that I am beginning to get worried about, and I can't get a straight answer."

"What are you playing with?"

"Opawica, New Brunswick Uranium, Joutel, and a bunch of other stocks related to the same deal."

I was astounded. These were companies in the stable of Vincent Noble Harbinson, a well-known Toronto promoter. He was, at the time, a desperate man. His then current wife had barricaded herself in the family's resort property at Lake Muskoka and was in the process of using the recently reconstituted family laws of Ontario to reformat her finances.

Although she had been a very short-term current wife, she did have a one-year-old child. As the Peter Nygard situation with the stewardess proved, this could be a winner. It was almost a cliché, with the aggrieved wife showing up in court with the little beastie attached to the breast and in tattered clothes while the cigar-chomping, skirt-chasing swine spent his nights in the arms of another man, woman, or whatever. The judges loved it. It was easy to understand.

But what to do when the little missus found out that her heart belonged to Mandy? The new family laws now did not even require that the husband be a scoundrel. He could still get shorn even if he were Saint Augustine. (He was the one who said, "Lord, please make me virtuous, but not yet.") In those days with the new family law the wife's lawyer would allow a reasonable amount of debit to build in the wife's account, being almost certain that she would prevail and his fee be paid. The husband's lawyers wanted cash on the barrel. They knew their client was doomed.

So Harbinson was feeding the local lawyers and trying to extract money from the market to do it. I encountered him while I was riding down the elevator of his Richmond Street office building. I was astounded to see with him his twenty-something son (the product of a much earlier current wife). Both of them returned my greeting but neither of them acknowledged the other.

That night, at the bar on the fifty-fourth floor of the TD building, I asked Peter, in a roundabout way, about the familial dissension. Apparently, Noble, in his desperation, had tampered with his son's mining promotion in such a manner as to extract a few dollars. My cronies at Hy's said the elder Harbinson merely wanted to sharpen his son's understanding of the pitfalls of mining promotion.

"Peter, you know how oil and gas comes from sedimentary rocks."

"Material laid down under water and containing some organic material. The stuff gets compressed and the organic material turns to hydrocarbons. Gas and oil."

"Right."

"Harbinson is drilling for gas in Michigan. Michigan is underlain by rocks of the Canadian Shield – granites, that sort of thing. Those are igneous rocks. No organic material – no hydrocarbons."

"Yeah, but Harbinson's geologist says that those rocks were originally sediments and have turned into what appear to be igneous rocks by heat and pressure. He says that at a depth of ten thousand feet the remnant gas will be there in size."

"Peter, that is a fairy tale. There are a dozen arguments as to why that can't happen. I haven't got all night."

"Shit. I didn't think it sounded real. Natural gas in igneous rocks. Wow, to think we believed."

I really felt sorry for them. Here were a bunch of stock jockeys caught in the clutches of a guy who a few centuries earlier would have been selling alchemy stocks. When Peter asked that I go and speak to their head honcho, Jim Connacher, I felt almost obligated. We arranged that Peter would get an alternate partner for next Wednesday afternoon's doubles squash game, and I would visit Gordon Capital after the market closed.

I kind of resented giving up the time, because I was busy on a research project. My ex-helper, Bob Buchan, had left Ames and gone over to the firm of Brown Baldwin Nisker as a mining analyst and then on to Ned Goodman's CMP Fund. This was a fund set up to hold flow-through mining shares on the behalf of investor. The fund would collect the write-off of exploration expenditures and "flow" these through to the investors, who would claim them as a tax write-off. Brilliant idea. As a result, Bob was approached by mining promoters wanting to sell their exploration credits to his fund and therefore heard about most of the deals going around. Bob had called me and said that two old-time mining promoters, Hughes and Lang out of B.C., had acquired some moose pasture near where Murray Pezim (yes, my old core-logging client) was drilling at Wawa, Ontario.

There were some great gold values in some old road cuts for the Trans-Canada Highway, and they were going to put some holes into these, drive the shares from the issue price of $2.50 to at least $5, and blow them off. Everyone but the suckers would make money.

I sometimes rode these deals. I never believed the target price would be reached and so, like Bernard Baruch, always sold just a little too soon. But this one was intriguing. The gold values in the roadway were half an ounce while at the time the mines in Timmins were mining quarter ounce. This was twice as good as the existing mines. I had taken an afternoon to explore the Ontario Bureau of Mines library at their then building on Alexander Street in downtown Toronto, and I had ordered from the Geological Survey of Canada all their material on the Wawa area. The information indicated that the area's geology was very similar to a Brazilian location that had been mined since the arrival of the Portuguese.

There were reported findings of good grade gold along a fairly continuous line. The host geology looked like they might have been old sedimentary rocks that had been altered to an almost igneous appearance.

The Engineers Club of Toronto was a mining hangout. I was a member and tried to have lunch once a week at the long table for unaccompanied members. There the local scuttlebutt would be tossed around. While at lunch I asked the then head of the Canadian exploration for Falconbridge, Stan Charteris, why there had never been any serious gold exploration in the Wawa/Hemlo area of Ontario.

"Model. Doesn't fit the Timmins model. If you want to find a viable gold deposit in Ontario it has to have some similarity to Timmins where the geological activity re-mobilized the gold and provided commercial concentrations. Those road-cut values are just paleo-nuggets. Good to promote with, unlikely to produce a real mine."

"But Stan, it hasn't even been used to promote a scam," I replied.

"Yeah. Look at what's going on. Murray Pezim has drilled over sixty holes in that Corona thing of his with no real results. All he has is just a bunch of scattered assays. Enough to get him drop-in-the-bucket financing. Every time the stock pops up, someone at this table will short the shit out of it."

The dichotomy of opinion arose from the fact that most of the guys at this table had graduated from Queen's or University of Toronto, and for them, nothing existed west of Manitoba. I had attended the University of British Columbia and had a much different attitude.

I thought about it. If Bobby Buchan was right and this was just a promotional play, I could blow the stock out at somewhere north of $4 a share and take $15,000 out of the market. I would buy ten thousand shares in my Registered Retirement Savings Plan at $2.50 a share so the gain would be tax free, and I would short a similar position in my own hands once the stock got over $5 (you couldn't short in an RRSP).

But what if my gut feel on this was right? There were gold showings along a well-defined line of rocks, always in the same rock type. This could be real. As well, there were, according to the maps, the long-held Williams claims. These had been held since just after World War II and passed on in the family. The Williamses had to be either convinced or crazy. Then there was Murray, the wild card. I wondered how he would feel if some twenty years later I was to show up at his core shack to do some midnight logging.

"Fellas, Murray Pezim has drilled about sixty holes into a property at Hemlo," I said. "What does that tell you?"

"It tells you he has a drill," Stan Holmes said.

I gave up on the dithering and bought ten thousand shares. The following day I met Jim Connacher.

III

Taking Charge of the Asylum

15

The Sheltered Workshop on Bay Street

O~N~ the appointed Wednesday I walked across King Street to the TD Bank tower. On the fifty-fourth floor was what had been Merrill Lynch's bond-trading operation. Merrill, after one of its many forays into the Canadian market, had retired once again to the safety of New York, leaving a nicely laid-out trading office as a cheap sublet. The Gordon guys were short on income stream, so this worked out perfectly. But I was about to have my first introduction to Gordon logic. The very attractive receptionist, Susan, asked that I not get any of my cigar ash on the carpet in the reception area, because it was very expensive.

"How expensive?"

"I think they paid around twenty-five thousand for it."

For that kind of money you should be able to get silk on silk, either Persian Qum or Turkish Harike. This was neither. It was a run-of-the-mill Afghanistani cotton on cotton probably worth a thousand. I was immediately struck by the old adage that salesmen are the easiest sell.

Then Jim Connacher came in and we each had a Scotch. He was a short man, well built, probably a year or two younger than I. He had a distinct air of intensity about him.

"Jim, what did you want to see me about?" I asked.

"We need a ranked analyst and I don't think Deacon is a place for a ranked analyst to make money."

"You think that Gordon Securities is?"

"Yeah. We've got no hang-ups about ethnicity or anything else. We're going to take over the institutional stock business."

"How so?"

"Facilitate the client."

Wow. This was unheard of. A broker was going to work for the person who actually paid him, the ... the client. I couldn't believe what I was hearing. I thought back on Martin in London who told me that an institution's first objective was self-preservation. But in a way he was still right. This was the ultimate way to preserve a brokerage firm: make the client need it.

At Ames and the rest of Bay Street, meanwhile, the client was a source of revenue. It reminded me of the famous question asked by a Midwestern farmer when shown the stockbrokers' yachts at their berths in the East River of New York: "Where are the clients' yachts?"

I felt uneasy because Gordon Securities had been going through people at an enormous rate, all in the space of two years: Jim Clubb, a well-known European salesman; John Lloyd-Price, a ranked oil-patch guy; and two mining analysts, Drago Samsa and Chris Thomson. Then there was also the recent departure of Monty Gordon and Gordie Eberts, the two founders. Pretty scary stuff. Also, when I had called around the street and asked about Gordon Securities, the main image I got was that it was unfocused. But there was something that didn't make sense. Peter Hyland.

What had Peter seen here that I couldn't see? He had joined and put up his own money (actually a lot of it was his farewell money from Osler), and as "Deep Throat" of Watergate fame said, "Follow the money."

Jim then led me into the trading area where all the salesmen and traders sat. It was tough trying to get into the room, it was so packed with egos. But as well, I didn't know if I had stepped into a geriatric ward or a wax museum. There were BSDs and big shooters scattered around like priceless antique furniture in an auction house. The youngest guy was at least thirty-five and there was only one. Everyone else, like me, was over forty. I thought, at first, that there should be a lawn-bowling court or solarium nearby for these guys but they were deadly serious.

And there was more than a whiff of testosterone in the air. It was past 5:30 p.m. The markets had been closed for over an hour, and these guys were still at the phones. The salesmen were talking to clients, and the traders were working with west coast brokers in Vancouver, Los Angeles, and San Francisco, where because of the time difference the markets were still open. From the frenzy I couldn't tell if it was desperation or dedication, but it was obvious these guys wanted to trade. I met some of the guys I didn't know and said hello to those I did. Peter, of course, was not there; he was enjoying a game of doubles squash. Had his ego been in the room, I definitely would not have been able to squeeze in with all the others.

I went home and over dinner with my wife and son mentioned that I had visited a brokerage that had no corporate-finance operation and no bond desk and where everybody seemed in a frenzy. They didn't even have a syndication department for new underwritings. My wife, the psychologist, attributed the frenzy to early attachment problems with their parents. My son thought that playing in the stock market was akin to a computer game and they were addicted.

During the night I tossed in bed wondering why all those other people had left. Or had they been pushed out? Maybe these Gordon guys didn't know what they wanted. Finally, I made my decision. I'd follow the money. It was unlikely you would lose doing what Peter Hyland did.

My departure from Deacon Hodgson was an unhappy event for me because I had acquired some good friends there. I knew I would have to give up going to New York with Rob Harris and London with Bob Acheson. But I also knew that there was money to be made in North America, and that Gordon Securities, as it was then known, looked like a good place to do so.

16

I Meet Groucho Marx

AT my first morning meeting at Gordon, at 8 a.m., I laid out what I had figured out about the Hemlo gold play. One of the salesmen told me he had heard from the analyst at Bunting (another small firm) that it was all a hoax. Frank Constantini, the trader, said, "What have you got to lose – $2.50 a share?" Frank was the only one with balls. The others were of the belief that the other guy's prophet could beat ours anytime. It was the Groucho Marx syndrome but in an information sense. Groucho had said, "I would never belong to a club that would have me as a member." The sales guys at Gordon could never believe an analyst who would work for Gordon.

My next bombshell was to dismiss the Michigan deep gas as a fairy tale. Tor Boswick jumped up and said I was just like all mining analysts: hidebound, uninformed.

"For God's sake, Doulis," Tor screamed. "Virtually all the sales guys at McDermid, Moss Lawson and Brandt, and all the other avant-garde firms are moving on this. You've got to get en courant."

The firms Tor had mentioned were all of the ilk that put their clients into questionable mining deals and then, when one paid off, took them out way too soon because they knew that anything they sold to their clients could never be any good. There was a dead silence in the boardroom as some of the lads started to digest what had been said.

"Isn't that what Zederynko said?" John Malowney asked. "I sold a shit-load of that to Manufacturers Life. You've got to be wrong."

Here it was again. Zederynko worked for us, so he couldn't possibly know the realities. But mind you, Wally Weekelbow, who had once been to Sudbury and vaguely knew the difference between theology and geology, was the man to listen to. I then realized what was going on. It was the story of the dentist from Owen Sound, the fabled schnook of the investment business.

In Ontario there were unregulated "broker dealers" who had the right to sell over-the-counter shares to the public. Because there was no real market, the prices were dictated by the market makers, who were the broker dealers. So if you phoned and asked the market on Wormwood Industries, the salesman at Bucket Shop Securities Inc. would quote you something like, "Offered at $1, bid $0.50." The shop was both a buyer and seller of the securities at their dictated prices. Here's how it would go:

"I'd like to bid $0.51 for a hundred thousand shares."

"You'll never get filled because the only offer is from our firm, Bucket Shop Inc."

"But what if someone wants to sell?"

"Then I will buy from him at $0.50."

"But what about my bid at $0.51?"

"Well there's nowhere to post that."

The story goes that the dentist from Owen Sound is phoned by Murray Shifty, a salesman at Bucket Shop Inc., and told of a fabulous new company that is developing technology to find subsurface gold using infrared and sound waves. Pharos Technology is the wave, and the shares are a paltry $0.75 each.

"I'll take ten thousand," says the dentist.

The next day the dentist calls Murray Shifty at Bucket Shop and asks, "What's Pharos Tech today?"

"The shares are being offered at a buck."

"Fabulous, I'll take another ten yards."

The weekend passes and the dentist can't wait to get to the phone on Monday. "Murray, how's Pharos Tech doing?"

"They're offered at two bucks."

You'll note that Murray Shifty is always quoting the asking price (the price that his firm is willing to sell the shares for) to the dentist, never the bid price at which the client might be able to sell, which may be non-existent.

"Son of a bitch, they've doubled over the weekend. Get me another ten yards, would you?"

The dentist can't believe his good fortune at Murray's having phoned him. The gods were smiling. But the dentist isn't greedy; he figures he's made at least a couple hundred thousand on Pharos by the end of the month. He phones Murray and asks, "What's Pharos this morning?"

"Offered at five dollars a share."

"Sell, sell. Sell it all. I'm rich."

"Sell? To whom?"

"To the market, Murray. Sell it into the market."

"I can't."

"Why, Murray? Why?"

"You are the market."

It was now apparent to me what had happened. Noble Harbinson had gotten through to somebody at Gordon (I later found it was Tor Boswick) and sold him the story. Tor had promptly sold some of the other guys, as salesmen are the best buyers, and the dance was on. When you went to the quote machine and looked at the amount of Opawica shares on offer and being bid for, you found that Gordon was the only real buyer. When you looked at the trading blotter, it was Gordon that had taken the shares from less than $4 to over $7. Yup, we were the market. Nobody could break ranks now or there would be a rout.

Malowney had stuffed the Harbinson company shares into Manufacturers Life and Tor to most of the senior executives at the old Cadillac Fairview Corporation. There were others, I am sure, but as I found out from Rick Betts, Manufacturers' mining guy, that when Manufacturers cut us off from any business for six months, it was because of the Harbinson company shares.

It was a rocky start and I wasn't sure I should unpack my files. But then I found out that after that morning meeting, Jim Connacher had instructed Frank Constantini to buy the first hundred thousand shares of one of the Hemlo companies I was recommending and then followed it with more. There were two superb junior companies in the best part of the Hemlo play, Golden Giant and Goliath. This was because promoters liked to spread property around so a number of their companies were in play all the time. Frank was now buying both for the firm.

By the end of the week the news was circulating in the firm that we had bought the Hemglo stocks for our firm's account and the first batch of deeper drilling assays had come in and were averaging about 0.40 ounces of gold to the ton. Spectacular! I had told the morning meeting that the rule of thumb in mining exploration was that the first three holes prescribed the grade of the deposit and then all the rest of the drilling was for tonnage. This could be big. The majority of the other brokers and analysts subscribed to the theory that this deposit didn't resemble the geology of the Timmins area and would therefore never make the big time.

That morning as I wandered past the sales desks I could hear the conversations between our guys and the clients.

"Yeah, I really like this Hemlo play. As I always say, the first three holes are for grade; now it's just a question of tonnage."

"I've been on this all along. I just didn't want to say anything until I had most of the facts."

"Sure it doesn't fit the Timmins model, but you know all paleo placers don't have to be deformed." This from a guy who an hour earlier thought that a deformed placer deposit had trouble walking.

"The analyst, Doulis? Yeah, he likes it, I think."

And then there were the prima donnas with their noses out of joint about Opawica who weren't going to even acknowledge my existence, not to mention buy my recommendation. I could see that I might not make any money at Gordon, but I would learn a lot from Connacher, Constantini, and Hyland. Also, I was going to have a lot of fun and many laughs.

17

Are they Stuffed or Waxed Models?

AS I mentioned, stepping into the Gordon trading/sales area on the fifty-fourth floor of the TD Centre was a startling experience. It was the Hockey Hall of Fame of investing, but the displays were still breathing.

There was Ron Goldsacks, the big scorer in New York; Geoff Green, the pipeline to the Reichmanns; Tor Boswick, who seemed to know all the real-estate tycoons in Canada; and Frank Constantini, one of the world's all-time great traders. I thought they were all dead, but in fact they were alive and well and hiding out at Gordon. To handle Montreal they had Derek Nelson, who knew where every last remaining dollar of the former financial capital was still hiding.

What clearly caught the eye was that this was a stock-trading operation. Every action and effort was dedicated to facilitating a trade. As a result it was the only true stockbroker in North America and probably the world. Oh yeah, I can hear you saying, what about Merrill Lynch, Wood Gundy, or Nesbitt Burns? In 1980 they should have been more accurately labeled as "stock agents" in the same way as "real-estate agents."

A broker is a person who buys from you and pays you from his funds and then attempts to sell what he has bought to someone else. An agent acts on your behalf to find someone to buy your asset and sell it, if he can find a buyer. So a real-estate agent will try to find a buyer for your house. In the pre-1980 days an investment dealer would try to find a buyer for your shares. This wasn't difficult if the size of your holdings was less than a thousand shares, but it became a chore if the size of the holding was ten thousand shares or more.

The way those large blocks were handled was that they would be shopped around until a buyer was found. So if you were a fund manager you could see the price of the Bell Canada shares that you wanted to sell at the then current price of $30 a share slide off to $25 as everyone in the business determined that your block was overhanging the market. Seeing that the dealer who did the trade was working with a fixed commission schedule, it didn't really matter who you did the trade with or at what price. There was one way to differentiate. The dealers provided free investment research to the community. Obviously the dealer whose research was consistently better than his competitors was of more worth to the fund manager and hence worth more business overall. Good research was the route to bigger market share.

In 1980 Hyland and Connacher decided that to garner more business the research had to be beefed up. They needed stars. So the ranks were thinned and new blood brought in that was highly regarded by the fund managers. I covered the mines, Ed Zederynko the oils, and Peter Hyland the steels. But that was only three of the fourteen subgroups of the Toronto Stock Exchange Index. Although business picked up, there was still a limit to what the fund managers could allocate as business to us based on our research coverage. Another weapon was needed.

You remember how I have been harping on the fixed-commission schedule. That no longer exists. It was murdered and left dying in Opera Lane behind the TD Centre. Gordon Capital was the culprit.

The smartest guy in the world noted that one of the advantages of being a member of the Toronto Stock Exchange was that you could buy and sell for your own account without having to pay commission. This was not only a courtesy, it was also a necessity. Some floor traders operated as a "box" on a stock offering to buy and sell the shares at fixed prices to maintain a stable market. This was similar to the "specialist" system used in New York. As well, during the period that a new issue was in distribution, a "box" had to be run on the shares to maintain an orderly market until the issue was sold. If commissions were paid on those market-stabilizing trades, the costs would become prohibitive. Therefore Gordon Securities could buy and sell for its own account without commission fees.

What would happen if, say, Manufacturers Life wanted to sell a hundred thousand shares of Bell Canada at $25? They would receive $24.90 per share if the transaction went through, and if the shares were bought by OMERS (Ontario Municipal Employees Retirement System) they would pay $25.10 per share. This was in order to facilitate the fixed-commission schedule. But let's say that Gordon Securities steps in and offers Manufacturers Life $24.95 per share net to them? Does that mean that Gordon has a client offering to buy the shares at $25.15? No, it means that Gordon is going to buy the shares for its own account and then find a buyer, probably OMERS, and sell them to the client at $25.05. Each client saves $5,000 on the trade. There's a slight problem. For Gordon to buy a hundred thousand shares of Bell from Manufacturers requires Gordon to put up $2.5 million, which at that time was one-third of its total capital. Therein lay the risk and the problem. With our limited capital, only a limited amount of trade could be facilitated.

They caught the old-time dealers flat footed. How was Gordon doing all these trades? Not only were they trading a lot of share blocks, but they were also doing a lot of them as crosses, which meant they had both sides of the trade, sell and buy. The brainiacs at the old-line firms were going crazy. Gordon couldn't be doing these trades as liability trades (buying for their own account), because they didn't have the capital. So how was this happening? They were taking over the market. There was panic. It was worse than if the market had fallen five percent in a day. The ethnics were taking over the market. A bunch of escapees from the geriatric wards of the city's hospitals had captured eight percent of the total volume traded and were going higher.

Once more brains triumphed over brawn. The big guys had the capital but were afraid to use it. Gordon had very little of its own capital but the smart traders to utilize what they had. What the big boys didn't realize was that Gordon seldom put up its capital, because they laid out a trade before they actually went to the seller or buyer. So once both sides had been found, the shares would be in Gordon's account for an instant, then gone before the nightly capital position was calculated.

18

Holy Smoke

ED Zyderynko had paid his dues. He had sat on drill rigs from the time his mommy first caught him smoking. Sitting on a rig is like logging core but from the soft-rock side of the geology business. Mines are found in hard rock geology and hydrocarbons in soft rocks, otherwise known as sedimentary rocks (irrespective of what V. Noble Harbinson may have claimed). There has to be a geologist on the drill site to record what is happening and to make decisions regarding what further work is required. Ed knew all the tricks.

While a hole is going down, something sticky in the drill-return water might be encountered. The geologist would order a test at the depth to determine if the goop indicated the presence of oil. If the stuff burnt, it meant hydrocarbons were present. If not – no joy.

So Ed would pay the scouts who hung around in the hills near where the drilling was going on to pass their observations on to him. Ed knew before the news release came out that a company was or was not having success in its program. All from the black smoke or lack thereof observed by the scouts. Energy was hot and Gordon was doing a grand business in trading the companies that were drilling in the far north. A lot of thought was going into calculating the value of all this oil, but nobody had stopped to think about how the average Canadian was going to fill'er up. The smartest guy in the world did.

Peter Hyland, a steel analyst, sat down with Zederynko and they figured out how big and how long a pipe it would take to bring the minimum amount of oil necessary for commercial production to Ontario. It would require a lot of steel. When Peter's steel report hit the street, the market went into a buying frenzy of steel stocks – so much so that the market regulators called Peter in for a chat. Peter proved to them that either the entire Canadian steel industry would have to be turned into one large pipe factory or the oil and gas in the Arctic as a producing entity was a result of someone's indulging in recreational pharmaceuticals. Sadly, it turned out to be the latter.

What I found bizarre in the whole incident was that Gordon Capital and Hyland were criticized for issuing a report about steel consumption based on the accepted wisdom that the oil and gas wells being drilled in the high Arctic were being undertaken to produce fuel for southern Canada and the US. The real hole in the thesis was the viability of Arctic energy. The Toronto Stock Exchange and the Ontario Securities Commission had no business criticizing Hyland's report if they did not question the viability of the Arctic-exploration ventures.

But it was the early 1980s and I was about to become an energy analyst as well. Remember those lineups at gas stations in the US?

When I lived in Utah I had the diversion of skiing in the winter, but what to do in the summer? Well, visit mining ghost towns in the environs, of course. Places like Park City where George Hearst, father of William Randolph Hearst, made his first fortune. I went to Virginia City, Nevada, where Hearst made his second fortune and a lot of others made their first. The interesting thing about Virginia City, besides its geology, was that the lawyers involved in the litigation between the companies made more in fees than the mines paid in dividends. Some things never change. But the geology was interesting and led to one of the major problems underground: the presence of hot, brackish water. So much flowed into the mines underground that new methods of pumping and ventilation had to be invented. That was 1858.

In 1981 Max Goldhar and Bob Faskins had control of a nice little producing gold-mining company called Camflo. It had a rather pretty treasury. The reason the treasury existed was that the directors of that era felt it was a socially bankrupt policy to pay dividends to the shareholders. If the shareholders were stupid enough to own shares such as Camflo's, who could tell what other foolishness they could get into given some free cash in the form of dividends? It was better for all concerned if the directors invested the excess funds generated by the corporation in something that could make some real money.

There was another consideration. Promoters, as you probably know, are not excited about production. What turns their cranks is a jump in the share price. If you are running a mining company, the share-price movement can most easily be brought about by exploration. In 1981, gold-mining exploration had been overshadowed by Hemlo, so the next best thing was energy. How can a mining company explore for energy? Well, if you're a big old mining company like Dome Gold Mine, you start your own oil and gas company and call it Dome Petroleum. If you are a tiny gold mining company, you drill for steam. No, I am not kidding. You find a steam mine. Or so Max and Bob would have you believe.

The phone rings with the pitch.

"Alex, I've got something hot for you and I mean that in two ways. You've heard of steam?"

"Max, of course I've heard of steam."

"Did you know that the entire Italian state railway system is powered by steam?"

"No, its not; it's electric."

"You don't understand, Alex. Where do you think the electricity comes from? Turbines that are driven by geothermal steam in northern Italy. And what about Iceland? The whole damned country runs on geothermal energy. You said in your 1974 uranium report that there was an energy crisis looming. It's 1981 and it is here."

"Okay, Max, steam's the thing. Where is this steam source you're going to utilize?"

"We've spudded a hole in Nevada. There are geothermal springs all around us."

"Max, isn't steam in that area brackish?"

"I doubt it, but even if it is we can clean it, run it through a turbine, and put the electricity into the Pacific Gas and Electric grid, which is just over a mile away."

I am sure you realize, as I did, that steam is not like coal, something you dig up and then wash before you send it out in the world. Steam has a very, very limited shelf life. But the dance was on. Max would call me every other day.

"Alex, we're down five hundred feet and still no faulting. This steam deposit is perfectly capped."

Two days later. "Alex, we're down eight hundred feet and the drill bit came up warm!"

Two days later: "Alex, mud, f—ing mud! There's mud on the drill bit."

What this was supposed to convey was that there was water down the hole.

Two days later: "Alex, this is it. Hot mud! Goodbye energy crisis."

I would turn to my quote machine as these reports were coming in and note that the price of Camflo shares had moved up between 20 and 30 percent by the time the information got to me. So I figured that the calls reporting progress were being made on a reverse Rolodex basis, starting at Zederynko and ending at Andrews. Doulis being closer to A than to Z, I would be one of the last recipients of a call. This put me at a disadvantage. Or did it?

When I explained to my partners that Camflo would have to build the world's largest thermos bottle to store the steam before cleaning, they concluded that a short-selling spate would be in order to take some of the pressure out of the situation.

There is a great irony to this story. Peter Munk, at about the same time, had bought control from Gary Last of a little oil-producing company called American Barrick. He then turned it into a gold company and started taking over marginal gold mines that produced only because of the then high price of gold, which would shut down once again when the price declined. When Goldhar and Faskins managed to bring Camflo into the near-death camp, Munk took it into Barrick. By acquiring Camflo, he had also acquired an experienced mining engineer, geologist, and mine accountant who then built Barrick into a blockbuster. If Max and Bob had just stuck to their knitting and run a gold mine, they would have been the multi-millionaires, because those three Camflo individuals would have found the wealth for them.

Poor little Camflo, shot to death with a ball of warm mud.

19

Whom the Gods Would Destroy ...

THE inscription "Whom the Gods would destroy, they first make crazy" is on some piece of nice Paros marble somewhere in Greece. The problem is that the statement is uncanny.

Gordon was making so damned much money that we had to celebrate. It was mid-1980 and the market was in a bit of manic rush. Share prices were high and Gordon was good looking. The old-time dealers were worried. Where would it end?

Gordon threw a party at the new Four Seasons Hotel that even made that hotel's staff gasp. The Peter Duchin Orchestra flown up from the US, bowls of black Beluga caviar sitting by bottles of frozen vodka as you entered. Verve Cliquot champagne was available by the bucket, and for the uncouth, hard liquor intravenously. Lobster or beef? Perhaps both?

But some of the refreshments were horizontal as well. Gordon's partners maintained a sailboat at the Queen's Quay yacht basin. The boat named G Force could be seen from the firm's offices on the fifty-fourth floor of the Toronto Dominion Bank building. During lunch, if you were in the office, it was common to look through the tripod-mounted telescope to see if the boat was bobbing, indicating that someone had just got lucky.

By the end of the year the reality of the markets had risen from the deep like an octopus and had strangled Gordon Securities. I looked at my cheques and they were consistently lower than the guarantee and profit-pool participations I had been pulling in at Deacon Hodgson. All I could get from my colleagues by the way of explanation was bafflegab.

The quiet, serious guy in the firm was Norm Carney. He traded options for us and helped hedge some of our positions. I asked Norm to have lunch with me. We walked over to the 54th Restaurant, now Canoe, which was next door to our offices.

"Norm, are you making any money?"

"Can't."

"I know we are in a bear market, but people make money in bear markets. Joe Kennedy did. Bernard Baruch did."

I was describing the careers of two of the US market's greatest speculators. Both had come out of the 1929 stock-market crash richer than when it started.

Norm chewed on this as well as a thoroughly buttered roll. Then he said: "They were like bisexuals. They can swing both ways. There aren't a lot of bisexuals around, either in bed or the markets. Most market players are optimists, which is only normal because the market has an upward bias. They only swing one way. I doubt that there is one guy in our bunch who can even think of shorting the market."

He paused, looked at the menu, and finally sat back in his chair, which told me he knew what he was having for lunch and he knew what he was going to tell me. "Alex, you know we are holding a number of positions that we're underwater on," he said. "I can't buy puts* as those would be exercisable at prices lower than we are seeing quoted. I can sell calls† but the market sentiment is negative and calls don't fetch much. We're screwed."

"Why can't we just blow off the positions and wait until the market turns around?" I asked.

"By the time we cleared the books we probably wouldn't have enough capital to stay in business. Alex, the model is flawed."

"What are you talking about?"

"Research has shown that the movement of share prices is random. You can't know if the next price that Bank of Montreal trades at is going to be higher or lower than the last price. When we take on a position it is impossible to say that the next trade will be at a higher price. So you can't beat the market. Over the long term you will make, in real terms, after inflation is

---

*A put allows an investor the right to sell shares to an investor at a
  predetermined price.

†A call allows an investor to buy from you a share at a predetermined price.

taken out, about six percent on your money if you invest in the US market and about four and a-half percent in the Canadian.

"Your liability-trading model is a great idea badly executed. If you are willing to go short as well as long you will probably break even, because share prices are random."

"Stock markets aren't random," I said.

"Really? Will the price of Bank of Montreal shares close up or down tomorrow?"

"Norm, that's unfair. Over the long term, the price will rise."

"Yeah, and in the long term, we are all dead, as Lord Keynes said. Have you read *A Random Walk Down Wall Street*?* The book makes a very good case that moment-to-moment share-price changes are random. We take moment-to-moment share positions by buying from our clients. When a client unloads a hundred thousand Bank of Montreal shares on us, does Frank Constantini know that the price will be higher or lower tomorrow morning? He can't."

"Supposing you're right. What can we do?"

"Change the model or get the hell out of the game."

"Norm, we can't change the model," I said. "No bank is going to back our share positions as a straight participation – lose or win. If a bankroller wanted to participate in share speculation, he would do it on his own. He doesn't need us. The only way we can finance this is with the system we have in place."

"Then give this up and get a real job."

"Norm, have you looked at our numbers? We're over eight percent of the total market volume in both share and dollar terms. We're tied for second place. I know we will be number one within six months. We have a real deal here. We can't just walk away from it. It's just a matter of time until we get the kinks worked out."

"Bullshit. You are in a variation of the classic Gambler's Ruin statistical play. You're like my Uncle Stanley in that you really believe in this fairy tale. He got the exclusive agency to distribute Skoda cars in 1950. I said to him, 'Uncle Stanley, how's the car business going?' He says, 'Kid, they're selling like hotcakes. I can't keep 'em in stock.'

"There were a number of unmentioned items in my uncle's fairy-tale

_____
*By Burton Gordon Malkiel.

description of his car business. First was that he couldn't keep them in stock because no more were being exported to Canada. Second was that the cars were selling so well because he was losing two hundred dollars on each one he sold. Uncle Stanley spent the rest his days sewing buttonholes at Tip Top Tailors.

"Like Stanley, we've got a lock on the business but we are losing money on the deal because we don't have enough capital to hold positions and we hold too many. We should be short as well as long."

"Norm, we can't just walk away. What are we going to do, turn off the lights and give the keys to the landlord?" This was a common phrase within the firm, heard as often as "facilitate the client."

"The first thing is to get some sustaining capital to keep us alive."

It was duck-hunting season in Manitoba and we managed to bag a golden goose.

20

We Learned from Dick Cheney

Except for US politicians, the shooting of one's friends while duck hunting is considered a serious breach of stream and field etiquette. However, we were desperate, and Ron Goldsacks and Jim Connacher went hunting in Manitoba and managed to bag Neil Baker. Neil had retired from working with the Bronfmans and for his efforts was allowed to buy a Winnipeg fuel company at a very acceptable price. Neil had a place in Winnipeg, a cottage on Lake Tahoe, Nevada, and an old friend named Jimmy Connacher. Neil was a contented man.

Jim came along with tales of unlimited wealth that were more akin to shooting fish in a barrel than shooting ducks in the air. Could any concept be simpler? You could get rich by undercutting the fixed-commission scheme of the Toronto Stock Exchange and do it legally. Now, Jim is an excellent salesman, and I am surprised that after he gave the sales pitch all three exited the duck blind alive. Had the armed individuals in that blind been more venal, I could see how they would have a shootout until only one remained to exploit this bonanza.

Also, Jimmy was like General Douglas Haig at the Somme in World War I. For Haig, throwing a few more thousand men at the Germans would be enough to tip the scales in the Allies' favour. Jimmy knew it would take only a few hundred thousand more dollars thrown into the jaws of liability trading to take over the market. Like the Canadian General whose troops Haig wanted to throw at the Germans, Neil Baker had his doubts. If this was such a money machine, why were the lads at Gordon Securities willing to give up a piece of it to some farm boy from Manitoba? Then the minor fact of a significant unsold inventory surfaced. Neil didn't have to shoot the other two men in the blind; they were already on their knees in full surrender.

So he threw $400,000 into the pot, which soon was gone. It was time to bring in the reserves or otherwise the previous mentioned amount was toast. So Neil ponied up $5 million and put strict controls on the inventory positions. We would no longer leave the office at night owning a significant percentage of the value of the shares on the Toronto Stock Exchange. Frank Constantini's dream of owning everything on the exchange and dictating prices to the buyers was gone.

But Neil brought more to the table than just some cash. Remember, he had worked for the Bronfmans. While doing so he met a nice South African chap who had worked for him. That was Jack Cockwell, who was soon to become the legendary head of a company with the ultimate deep pockets, Brascan.

Neil's connection to Brascan was our secret weapon. We started buying positions from our clients with Brascan's money. Brascan would take 20 percent of the profit and none of the loss if we mis-stepped. We now had infinitely deep pockets with which to work. However, there was something troubling me. First was a deal whereby you bring an investor into a trade and guarantee him that he won't lose money. Call your broker and ask him if he will do that for you. I was worried that if the Ontario Securities Commission found out about our arrangement, embarrassing questions might be asked. Even today where the banks are financing their in-house trading desks, I wonder how those agreements with respect to profits and losses are structured to get around the rule of not being able to offer the client a risk-less trade.

Even more troubling was how would we make money in a new environment where we had to give away 20 percent of the profit. We were hardly getting by when we were able to keep 100 percent of the profit. Think of it this way. Tossing a coin is a random event. Fifty percent of the time you have heads and 50 percent tails. If you bet a dollar on the outcome being heads and play over a long time, you have to break even, because you win half as many as you lose. But what if every time you win you give $0.20 to a third party but every time you lose you pay the full dollar? Eventually you're broke.

However, my history was catching up with me once again.

21

The Mouse Killers

IN my happy youth as a geologist I had worked at times for the renowned firm of mining consultants, Chapman, Wood and Griswold, of Tucson, Arizona. They were the firm of choice of Vernon F. Taylor III, who, during the 1950s and 1960s, controlled Placer Developments, as it was then known. Placer's vice president of exploration at the time was Ed Scholtz.

I had met Ed on occasions and was impressed, as I was with most of the talent at Placer. Ed was fascinated by open-pit mining and brought into production the Endako molybdenum mine in central British Columbia even though his detractors said no mining method could be derived to produce from the deposit because of its low grade. He made it work and produced a bonanza for Placer. When Ed retired he went back to his roots in Montana and looked at a property there that had been closed down for years. It was the old Montana Tunnels gold property near Bozman.

Ed was also fascinated by something he had seen at my old employer, Kennecott. When Kennecott stripped the low-grade copper-bearing material overlaying the ore at its enormous open pit in Bingham Canyon, Utah, it stockpiled the material on concrete pads. The company would then spray dilute acid on the piles. As the acid trickled through the heaps, it dissolved the minor amounts of copper present. Upon coming to the pad drainage system, the solutions would encounter all manner of iron oxide in the form of tin cans and other steel debris from which the tin or any other coating had been burned off. The solutions would react with this, precipitating the copper and adsorbing the iron. Kennecott was literally leaching the copper out of the heaps of low-grade material. Note that the cost of extracting the copper in this method is minimal because the mining cost was paid for by the ore processed through the mills.

Ed was a lateral thinker. If you could heap leach copper, why not gold? He started a new company, Pegasus Gold Inc., with the Montana Tunnels property, which had been an underground gold mine, and began stripping off the surrounding rock and leaching it. It produced gold but the grade at Montana Tunnels was less than .07 ounce to the ton so that at $600 per ounce it was a dollar-trading operation, never really making an economic profit. But still, it worked; the only problem was that the grade was too low.

Ed knew of some properties near the old Homestake Mine in the Black Hills of South Dakota. They had been underground mines that produced ore of about .15 ounces per ton. Whenever the grade fell to .1 ounce or less, the material was left behind, and there was lots of it. To finance the deal he went to a Canadian natural resource conglomerate, Coseka Resources. They financed Ed's new heap-leaching deal, Wharf Resources. Ed put his son, Dan, in as mine manager and started the operation, improving on what he had learned in Montana. It looked like it was going to work. However, Ed died in a car accident before the venture really proved itself.

Gordon had sold control of Coseka to Bramalea, a real-estate company. That's partially true. We actually sold it to both Bramalea and Teck. When the day of delivery arrived, Jim Connacher had to advise the buyers that it had inadvertently been sold twice and a flip of a coin would have to determine the winner, or as some might say, two losers. Bramalea wanted the oil production in Coseka and weren't thrilled to have the mining assets in the package in the first place. With the guiding light behind this new mining method dead, they wanted out of the mining assets. After they had unsuccessfully tried to sell their thirty-two percent holding in one of the mining companies, Wharf Resources, they came to us, the people who had sold them the package.

Sell Wharf, they said.

Jim Connacher dropped the file on my desk and told me to find a buyer. As I went over the data I could see that this was going to be a real winner. The largest piece of any of the deals that Ed Scholtz was involved in was his holding of Wharf. Ed believed in it. Also, the highest-grade gold waste in North America of any size was in the Wharf holdings.

I went to see the property. As I was driven around by Dan Scholtz, Ed's son, he asked me to keep a watch for dead mice.

"That's an odd request, Dan. What's up?"

"The mice are very susceptible to the cyanide leach solutions we use and if they get at it, the environmental people conclude that we aren't recovering all our leach solutions. These guys get upset if we kill the mice. But what's worse is that the solutions are full of gold and we don't get to process the mice. The environmental guys keep them."

There was another, more pressing issue. The Lead, South Dakota, mines produced from a very fractured group of rocks. At those fractures there had been movement grinding up the rock in the fracture and producing mud. The mud was gold-bearing. But the mud would not fall off the buckets of the machinery used to spread the crushed rock on the heaps. More importantly, it fouled the crusher. All that was needed was a dryer at the crusher site and all their problems would be over. Dan told me that $9 million would solve the problem.

When I reported this to my colleagues, they immediately came up with a $24 million issue of 8.5 percent convertible debenture issue as a solution to a $9-million problem. I could see erring on the side of caution but this seemed extreme. The Wharf board accepted the idea.

Bramalea had beat up the share price of Wharf in their attempt to offload the shares, so it was not surprising to see the shares take a momentary down dip just as the price at which the conversion feature was prescribed. As I remember, it was $2.25 per share. When the deal was announced, I thought what a great deal for investors. It asked.

While I was looking at the prospectus, Jim Connacher came over. "Alex, can you sell some of this new Wharf convertible?" he said.

"Can the Pope say mass in Italian?" I replied.

I didn't know if Connacher was black Irish, that is, Catholic, but I liked to throw a little disrespect at him in any case. I had just finished selling some to André Michaels in Switzerland when Jim ran, yes actually ran, over to my desk.

"What are doing?" he yelled. "I told you sell some of the issue, not the whole thing. Stop. Anyone who isn't firm gets none."

I now understood why the issue was such a good deal for investors and so large. We were the investor!

At $24 million, and with a small public participation, we could price the issue at the end of the day at whatever price we wanted. In this way we could inflate our asset base for capital calculation purposes. "Yes sir, Mr. Regulator, those Wharf resources really are worth $1,200 a piece. Just look at the market." As well we were getting a sweet yield and effectively a call on the price of gold. If the price of gold went up, the price of Wharf shares would climb to well above their current price and our conversion feature would be golden. Also, by virtue of the conversion feature, we could control the company. Wharf was eventually taken over at a price around $13 a share some eight years later.

The success of Wharf led to an interesting meeting with Bobby Friedland, ex-orchardist and one-time dabbler in recreational pharmaceuticals. He had concluded that mining promotion was the field that best suited his capabilities. Having spent time in California, Bobby was high-tech inclined and high tech had come to mining in the form of – yup you guessed it – heap leaching of gold ores.

A little research on Bobby's part would have informed him that the guy he was going to see at Gordon Securities (me) was the first one to merchant-bank a gold heap–leaching operation. Had he done so he might even have chosen to avoid making the call.

"Hi, I am Bob Friedland. You probably don't know that Steve Jobs and I grew organic apples in Oregon. Yeah, that's why he named the computer thing 'Apple.' We were very close."

I don't know if you're confused by that opening salvo but I sure was. I knew that this visit was about mining. Bob had said so on the phone. But was Steve Jobs getting into mining? Was there a connection between Apple computers and mining? Where they running out of silicon for the chips in Silicon Valley? I waited, awestruck, for the next utterance.

"The old days of ore processing are over. High tech is the way to go. I'll bet you've never heard of heap leaching for gold extraction. It's the new wave and it's going to make conventional mining obsolete. No more grinding and flotation cells and all that expensive crap. We can today mine lower gold grades than ever thought possible and process them to extract the gold at costs that seem inconceivable."

"But Bob —"

"Wait, you haven't heard the best part. Galactic Mines, my company, has locked up the best low-grade gold deposits in America. They're in Colorado."

"Wait, Bob —"

"No, there's no time to wait. This is the opportunity of a lifetime. Just look at these spreadsheets. Look at those production numbers. This thing is expandable to double or even quadruple the size because grade is not a limiting factor."

"I've got it," I said. "You're telling me that this new method is going to cause an upsurge in gold production worldwide causing a glut and I should sell all my bullion holdings."

I was just kidding him along because he was so earnest in his pitch that I thought some reinforcement, no matter how ridiculous, would be in order. "I can see what you're getting at," I said. "This new lower-cost production method is going to flood the world with cheap gold. The price is going to collapse."

"No, no. Look at this spreadsheet. Galactic is going to spit out money."

I looked at the numbers and noticed that Bob had shown twelve months of production per year. "Bob, where in Colorado is this mine?" I asked. "Is it in the mountains?"

"That's the joy of it. It's on a mountain top. Virtually no stripping."

"How high?"

"About ten thousand feet."

"Bob, doesn't water freeze at that altitude in the winter?"

"Yeah. So?"

"You've shown year-round production. How will the leaching solutions circulate in the winter when they're frozen?"

"They won't freeze."

I was really interested now because at Wharf Resources we found the gold production dropped off through the cold months because of freezing. If Galactic had a method of keeping the pads doing their leaching through the cold months, we should apply it.

"Bob, how do you stop water freezing at below-zero temperatures?"

"We have a secret process."

"Can you tell me what it is?"

"Alex, if I told you then it wouldn't be secret."

Bob had not thought of the other applications of his secret process.

World War II had been fought for a good part of the time in the winter on frozen ground. When the spring came and the ground thawed, fighting slowed to a crawl. Friedland's process of keeping water liquid at below zero would allow generals to stop advancing enemy armies in the winter by just melting the frozen ground between them and their opponents. The possible applications of Friedland's magic swirled through my mind. And here he was about to waste it on a heap-leaching mine at ten thousand feet.

Bob never did commercialize this anti-freeze process. The Galactic Mine collapsed with a $26-million environmental bill, and he left the scene faster than the speed with which I threw him out of my office.

22

We Are Our Enemy

THE firm was starting to get a reputation not just as a trading house but also as a deal house. If you wanted to get something done discreetly, then Gordon was the place. So how about a bunch of Jews wanting to sell hotel properties to a bunch of Arabs? You don't want that kind of information being blabbed around the synagogue or mosque, do you?

We were asked to look at the deal from the vendor's side while a stunning young lady with a mind that made you forget her looks represented the purchasers. I was asked to look at the deal by our firm. When I first met her she was wearing a gorgeous Burberry skirt, a Hermès blouse, and an Ivy League MBA. I had invited her to our boardroom because there was a participant in the transaction I could not assess. It was a company in Curacao. I asked my counterpart about it, and she said that we could never know who owned the company. What about banking? They bank in Guernsey, which has complete bank secrecy, was her answer.

My mind was running riot with this information as to the possibilities for the firm and me. Gordon was a partnership and as such all the partners were liable for the debts of their fellow partners. To make things worse, our partnership operated in a risky business. It was at this point that Tor Boswick walked past the open door of the boardroom. He didn't notice the young woman's MBA but he was struck by the endless legs starting at well-turned ankles.

I hope, dear reader, that you've been keeping a roster of the Gordon team, but if not let me remind you that Tor Boswick covered a clutch of retail clients that were large enough to be counted as institutions. His now ex-wife had taken offence at his activities at a party they were throwing at their (now her) residence.

Heartbroken from this event, and by now several years out of wedlock, Boswick fell into the arms of Susan, our receptionist. That actually requires some clarification.

To begin with, Gordon's ladies were picked as much for their feminine pulchritude as for their typing skills. Stiletto heels trumped typing. To appease the wives (remember these were all middle-aged men), there was a rule in the firm that there was to be no fishing from the company pier. This of course was obeyed more in the breach than the observance. My wife, upon meeting Boswick, said to me, "Never leave me alone in a room with that man." The man's effect on women was staggering. When we would go to Errol's Jazz Bar, the other lads would throw their Ferrari keys on the bar. Tor would stand at the door and run his hands through his salt and pepper hair. He would then walk up to some sweet young thing, lock his eyes onto hers, while she kicked her resistance, conscience, and morals under the bar as quickly as possible.

The romance with Susan was torrid. However, Tor was a teetotaler and only went to bars to socialize. Susan liked a nip and loved jazz. One day when Errol, the owner of the bar, blew his saxophone in the presence of Susan, her paramour's eyes were out and the barkeep's lips were in. Tor was devastated. One of the world's great stick men had been laid low by a publican, an itinerant musician. It was too humiliating.

But then that fateful day he passed the open door of the boardroom and there I was with – her. Susan fell away and Ms. MBA became the girl of his dreams. He walked into the room and asked for an introduction.

As he locked his eyes on hers, I thought, she's too smart for this. Instead, within minutes, I was reminded of a poem by the sixth-century BC poetess, Sappho:

> Desire shakes me once again,
> here is that melting of my limbs,
> It is a creeping thing, and bittersweet.
> I can do nothing to resist.

Okay, so I was wrong. They started a nuclear-powered relationship with both of them living within doors of each other on a trendy downtown street in Toronto's Hazelton Lanes. Invitations went out for hearthside dinners at her place, where she proved even MBAs could be gourmet cooks. There was talk of wedding bells, and I thought Tor might even take up white wine. But then, to paraphrase a World War II warning, "Loose Hips Sink Ships." In this case the hips belonged to Susan. Remember the beauty who dumped Tor for the sax player? She came back, but for a one-night stand only, because Errol had found a new band groupie and she was lonely. It would just be for old times' sake before Tor moved further down the aisle to matrimony.

She awoke the following morning as pregnant as a spring doe.

News, like tummies, spread fast in these circumstances. Soon Tor's true love was completely informed. Unlike the Curacao company's funds and bank that troubled the both of us, she knew exactly where this deposit came from.

23

The Deal's the Thing

THE Wharf issue was, at the time, one of the few corporate-finance deals we did. The reason being that the establishment boys in the big firms were still smarting over how our liability trading action was taking down the fixed-commission system. We were therefore offered few, if any, participations in any of the syndicates for good new issues. Then someone put it together. We had effectively bought all of the Wharf issue. Why not buy all of some other new issue and sell it to the public?

The smartest guy in the world was director of research and asked me if I would look into what happened when a new stock issue came out. I analysed the previous ten years and found that, on average, the price of a stock fell by fourteen percent from the time an issue was announced to the time the new shares were sold. So if the company's shares were selling at $100 today and tomorrow you announced a new issue, the price at the time the issue was finally done would be $86. The new shares would sell at $86 each and within three months return to something closer to the $100 level.

This was a great deal for everybody but the issuer. The broker was ostensibly working for the issuer when a new share position was offered, but in reality he was working first for himself and secondly for buyers. Screw the issuer. He has no alternatives. If he wants new shares in the market, then come to us and we will do the issue for him. The remarkable thing was that the investment dealers didn't even guarantee any performance. "Oh, sorry, Mr. Canadian Tire, we tried to sell your shares to the public at $25 each but only managed to find buyers for half of them. Oh what to do? Better luck next time."

Here's how a new share issue for an existing company was done.

First week: Preliminary Prospectus issued. No prices for the new shares, just the description of the issue and the company.
Second week: Green Sheet. Prices and terms suggested. Ask for expressions of interest from buyers.
Third week: Syndicate formed among the dealers. Those with the largest expressions of interest get the largest syndicate positions unless other factors, such as old favours, golfing buddies, or prospective in-laws, prevail.
Fourth week: Prices and terms set, final prospectus published, and sales effort begins.

Now, if you are a rational investor and you see at week one that there is a new issue of Bell Canada to hit the market, are you going to step up and buy in the market? You know that there is going to be some discount to market, so you wait. Some large investors figure they should sell their existing positions because they can replace the position at a lower price. So there are lots of sellers and few buyers. What happens? No, there isn't a pile of Bell Canada shares swept up into a corner on the floor of the Toronto Stock Exchange. The price drops.

So the corporate-finance officer from Mega Brokers phones Mr. Bell Canada and says, "Well, looks like your stock hit a new fifty-two-week low just as we are going into this new issue. To get you the hundred million you are seeking, we will need to sell another fourteen percent more shares. Odd, that."

"You're telling me that from the day I called you the issue is costing me fourteen percent?"

"Not quite. You see, there are our fees of seven percent, and don't forget the lawyers."

To make things worse, the sales syndicate might not even manage to sell the $100 million of shares offered, and Mr. Bell Canada has to deal with his financial needs somehow or other.

24

The Passing of A.E. Ames

I was having my own problems, and a serious death had occurred on Bay Street. It was 1981, and A.E. Ames had died.

Not the man – he died in 1934 – but the firm. Its finances were so bad that it was taken over by Dominion Securities (now RBC Dominion). So bad was the situation that instead of the usual two names of the firm being on the letterhead after a merger – Dominion Ames or some such thing – it was just Dominion. It was a complete takeover. Shares in Ames that at one time were trading privately at over $35 were being bought at picayune levels.

In less than a century Ames had gone from being the largest investment dealer and underwriter in Canada to being a shell. During my tenure there I could not have conceived of the idea that something as strong and power-ful as Ames could ever succumb. But then I guess the Emperor Augustus thought that of Rome, as did Fredrik Eaton of Eaton's and the people of Canada of the Hudson Bay Company.

The investment business in Canada was changing. The old loyalties were being pushed aside as the small dealers made inroads to the estab-lishment business. And the amounts of capital to do the big deals whether trading or underwriting were increasing, as were the risks. Also, there were new capitalists on the block who had no loyalties to the old dealers. The Reichmanns were doing financings through Bell Guinlock. That firm's Bob Canning brought them an innovative financing idea – to use bond issues to finance their real-estate ventures instead of bank financing – and they implemented the approach through him. Joe Pope took his clients into an investment in Algoma Railways that became a winner when he slapped Canadian Pacific Railway's wrist for selling Algoma assets, which they didn't own but only leased. Not only did Pope win the case, but the stock soared to new heights and made a lot of people richer.

25

I Didn't Know What Time It Was

A.E. Ames as a firm may have passed on to the great exchange in the sky, but I was on a roll. The Hemlo stocks the firm had bought quadrupled, our gold-leaching deal in South Dakota was pouring metal, and new Ferraris were being added to the Gordon partners' stables. I decided to take the new wife skiing in Switzerland and spend like the BSD I thought I was. There was also some tag-end business to take care of since my coal-handling days. So off we went.

Everybody at Gordon wore a Rolex watch. They had to because it was the most advertised of the high-end wristwatches. If Ron Goldsacks threw his Ferrari keys on the bar at Errol's Jazz Bar and a Piaget or Omega showed beneath the shirt cuff, the whole exercise would have been in vain. I had neither a Ferrari nor a Rolex and no intention of acquiring either.

I did however, as befits a man of significance in the investment industry, get myself fitted for a bespoke bicycle. I had a touring bicycle fitted at the old Bicycle Sport Shop on King Street. It was a thrilling experience to have a bicycle frame actually manufactured to fit one's anatomy, although I was not asked whether I "dressed on the right or the left" as my tailor inquired.

Having moved upscale in transportation, I now felt it was time to do the watch thing. Obviously the Rolex was out because everybody in the firm had one, including the messenger who made money by investing in what was happening on the trading desk. A watch is the only piece of jewelry that a man wears, so the choice is critical. Being in Switzerland for skiing, I was surrounded by jewelers. This simplified the problem.

One day as I was passing some time in Lausanne, I saw a Patek Philippe in the window of a shop. It had a fine gold link bracelet and cost twice as much as the priciest gold Rolex I had seen. It was love at first sight.

When I arrived in Toronto I contemplated having the left sleeves of my suit jacket shortened to provide a better view of my trophy. My tailor pointed out that I would have to have the left sleeves of my shirts shortened, as well, and that the resulting appearance would make me look somewhat deformed.

I had to somehow get my watch noticed with no sartorial assistance. It had to be by guile.

Every morning we had a meeting lasting till 9 a.m. to discuss the forthcoming day's events and our strategy for the trading session. It was imperative to end this on time so we could all get to work. On my first morning back from Switzerland, with my magnificent watch properly placed, I leapt up from my place at the boardroom table, swung my arm prominently around so as to put my wrist at eye level, and announced, "It's nine; let's go."

Nothing. No nice watch, great gold, or swell timepiece. Nothing. Variations on the theme of time telling and announcing went on for a week, but no one noticed. I had all but given up. However, one day out on the trading floor where the action started at 9:30, someone yelled out: "Anybody got the correct time? Are we trading yet?" I was standing beside Jim Connacher and before I could raise my arm to show my watch and report the exact time, he was looking down at the watch on his wrist. A Mickey Mouse watch. "Mickey's little hand is past nine and his big hand just at six," he said. "It must be 9:30."

"No," came another voice. "Mickey's big hand is past six so the market must be open."

Another voice: "You're both wrong. Mickey's big hand has not quite reached six."

They got me, and they got me good.

Trying to upstage my colleagues at Gordon was only one of many problems, one of which was closer to home.

26

Hello Angelo

WE had obtained a new home phone number. Regrettably, it had been the number of the Greek moving company Angelo Movers. The number had been changed in the white pages of the phone book but not in the yellow pages. We would get calls at odd times from some angry Greek-speaking person demanding to speak to Angelo personally. The calls were so frequent as to overflow the answering machine. Saturdays we could seldom sleep in because the calls for Angelo would start coming in as early as 8 a.m. It was maddening. Thankfully, I speak Greek fluently and could redirect the calls, but after a couple of months of telephone tyranny, I snapped.

It was 9:15 a.m., on a Saturday.

"Yes?"

"Angelo Movers?"

"Yes."

"You said you would be here at nine to move my furniture."

"I'm not coming."

"You have to. My lease ends at noon."

"Too bad."

I was about to put the phone down, but the Greek lady was almost in tears. "Why aren't you coming?" she asked.

"I don't work on Saturdays."

"Why not?"

"I am Jewish."

"But you speak Greek."

"Yes, I am a Greek Jew."

"You can't be. There's no such thing."

"Lady, I know what and who I am. I can't work today. Accept it."

"You'd better speak to my husband."

A male voice: "Hello, hello, Angelo?"

"Yes."

"My wife says you are not coming today because as a Greek Jew you don't work on Saturdays."

"A Greek Jew? Me? I've never heard of such a thing. It's impossible. You know that. You should have a talk with your wife. She's not functioning."

I hung up. During the following month the number of calls for Angelo Movers diminished to eventually nothing. The word had spread through the Greek community that there was a Greek out there who could not eat a pork souvlaki for religious dietary considerations, someone obviously to be avoided.

But the Greek thing kept getting me into trouble.

I was still one of the most trusted analysts covering Denison Mines, so I kept my coverage as complete as possible. I had noticed, in the recent quarterlies and annual report, that production from the company's Prinos oil field in Greece was becoming erratic and declining. I called Chuck Parmalee at the company and got a non-answer. Nobody in Canada could give me any answers. So I called Athens and talked to some people in the government's natural-resources area. They told me that the field had peaked and that there was about a three-year rundown in production coming. I published the results and recommended the sale of the shares.

I could hear my name being scratched off the Dension Christmas–party list up and down the Bay Street Canyon. When they found out that my information came from the Greek government, Denison had their solicitors, Fraser & Beatty, send me a letter. If I didn't cease and desist inquiring into the company's affairs in Greece, the company would bring the full force of the law to bear on me. After reading it I thought they were spitting into the wind, but I was still a little worried that a law firm would take the time to write such drivel if there was nothing they could do. I was doubly concerned because Gordon Securities didn't have much of a track record in protecting its employees. My fears were annulled by Tubby Black. Yup, the same one of Hollinger fame.

We – Jim Connacher, Conrad Black (pre-titular days), and I – were in the Gordon boardroom. At one point Steve Roman's name came up, and Jim mentioned that I had been receiving threatening billets doux from Dension's lawyers.

"Alex, may I see the letter?" Conrad Black said.

"Sure. It's on my desk. Hold on."

I returned and handed him the letter.

"Hmm. Harrumph. Hmm. Alex, you made this inquiry by phone?"

"Yeah, I came in early. There's a six-hour difference."

"You instigated the call?"

"Of course. There's no reason for them to be calling me."

"And when you spoke, what language were you using, Greek or English?"

"Those civil-servant guys don't speak English, so we spoke Greek."

"Well, Alex, this conversation would be judged by the courts to have taken place in Greece. Fraser & Beatty and their full force have no jurisdiction over phone conversations occurring in Greece. I suggest you place this letter next to the toilet."

It was later that I learned that Black had studied international law. I never thought at the time that some evolutionary throwback and mentally deprived aspirant to sordid, higher, political office, as Black would have described his current opponents, would ever think of taking on this guy.

The other problem I was having also concerned Denison. I was close to the financial guys at Dome Mines. During the great uranium boom of the 1950s, Dome had tried to take control of Denison Mines and been unsuccessful. They ended up with ten percent, or 1.75 million shares. They held the position until February 10, 1983, when I sold it. At the time it was the largest trade done on the Toronto Stock Exchange, and it was a cross. Which meant we did both sides of the trade: buy and sell. For that trade, which netted the firm over $6 million (and even more in the trading account), I received $65,000, or one percent, while even finder's fees were at least five percent. So if someone had brought the idea to Gordon, they would have made five times as much as I did. For the Wharf deal I had received nothing except my pool participation. I realized I was not going to get rich at Gordon. But then few people did.

But it got the brain trust thinking. We had bought the large remnant part of the Wharf debenture issue. What if we had bought the whole issue and sold some of it off? Same thing. You might say we underwrote the issue as real underwriters. You know, buy the new issue from the client and distribute it. We had bought the entire Dome position of Denison Mines and done a secondary issue.*

---

*A secondary issue results from the sale of a large or controlling position in a company's shares from the dominant or controlling shareholder to the public. Probably one of the worst investments you can make.

27

New York, New York

Ron Goldsacks, or Goldie as we called him, was the king of New York as far as Canadian brokers operating in that city were concerned. For example, he threw a dinner at the Normandy Hotel one night in the winter of 1982 to have me speak to US investors about the new Hemlo find and about Wharf Resources' new gold-production method. It started snowing at noon and got worse through the day of the dinner. I arrived at the Normandy at 5:30, to be greeted by an empty room. By 6:30 it was standing-room only. On another occasion, he hauled me out of downtown, the financial area, all the way up to midtown, 70th and Madison.

As we entered the office I noticed it was a mezzanine in a kind of greenhouse. The receptionist was an elegant-looking young man. When Goldie introduced himself, the receptionist called through to his boss's secretary, and another nice-looking lad, beautifully coiffed and attired, came out to lead us into the inner sanctum. I saw not one woman. Okay, I thought, this is midtown, so more pastels, fewer pinstripes. All the girls want to be downtown with the BSDs. We met Lou and he offered us tea. I gave him my pitch. When we left and were in the limo on the way to the hotel, I asked about the strange environment.

"For God's sake, Doulis, can't you see he's queer?"

"Wow, Goldie, I've never met a homosexual portfolio manager."

"Where do you think all the hairdressers, window dressers, male dancers, and drag queens go when they want to invest? You know, some of those guys turn big bucks."

"Why doesn't he deal only with gay brokers?"

'Two problems. First, how many bent brokers do you see? And second, pragmatism. There's another smaller guy servicing, or should I say investing, for this crowd, but Lou does the lion's share. He's got the better performance. He runs over $300 million."

"So, Goldie, you found the inroad to the homosexual money. Will be seeing the lesbians on our next trip?"

Goldie looked out the window. "No, the Episcopalians," he sighed.

Most people find New York frantic. After the Gordon offices I found it serene. There was none of the manic-depressive behaviour of people living on the brink of bankruptcy. When markets were roaring, so was the Gordon crowd. A couple of down days brought panic. Things were so erratic that the accounting staff couldn't figure out how much to withhold for our quarterly income tax payments. Some of the traders were well behind in their income taxes and on the wall we had a picture of a flasher exposing himself as seen from the rear. Coat open, trousers cut off to the knee. The caption read, "What John Malowney does when the taxman calls." The tax collectors called weekly during the first two months of 1983.

I had just finished a morning of calls and returned to our office at 49th and Park where a message was waiting for me to call Ian Mellon.

"We've merged with Daly," Ian said.

"Well, that's grand. How much did they bring to the table?"

"The estimate is nine million dollars."

"God knows we need it."

"Alex, there's more to the story. What is Daly known for? Their floor coverage. They have the most traders on the exchange floor of any of the firms, including the majors. We now control the trading floor."

There was a system known as high closing. When people with vested interests in share prices, such as mining promoters, wanted a good price printed in the morning paper for their shares, or people wanted to show inventory to their bankers, they would have the market "dressed" at the close. If you had good trading floor coverage, therefore, you made sure that all the positions you held in inventory closed at the best possible prices by buying all the board lots available at the close. It didn't take the purchase of more than a few hundred shares to make things look rosier.

But there is an irony to this event. Gordon decided to dissolve the retail operations of Daly that dealt with the man on the street. It just faded away to other firms. A smarter decision would have been to find some way to keep it going, probably as a wholly owned subsidiary. It was valuable, and four years later Gordon was trying to take over Wood Gundy to obtain a retail operation that would make Gordon saleable to a bank.

28

Gimme the Share Certificate

THE fixed-commission system was laid to rest by the Toronto Stock Exchange sometime around 1983 or 1984. It didn't make sense anymore because the other dealers had been forced into liability trading where the broker bought the share from the client for resale. However, after a few missteps where the old-time dealers found themselves with naked shorts (stock sold that they couldn't deliver) or long (some piece of merchandise somewhat cheaper than what they bought it for), it was time for a reassessment of the situation.

The feeling among the establishment dealers was that they didn't want to have to compete by buying blocks of shares. The exchange, ever willing to do the bidding of its owners, abolished fixed commissions, which meant that the other firms could offer the same sort of spreads that Gordon was offering without having to buy the position from the clients beforehand.

We breathed a sigh of relief, for two reasons. First, we no longer had to go to Hees or Brascan to back a really big trade. And second, we were released from having to gamble on the holding of large positions. As well, we had fifteen percent of the volume of the exchange (with a full roster of fifty-eight support people, if you included the waiter). And we had control of the trading floor as a result of our deal with Daly. It took the competition fifty people just to operate their secretarial pool, and they didn't have our floor coverage.

Without a fixed-commission schedule, the only losers were the old-line firms. Mansions in Rosedale began to look a little unkempt; the trade in up-market sailboats fell off; and the Muskoka Lake resort properties were marked back in price. All the toys of the establishment brokers were taking a hit. The market for Ferraris, however, was on a steady climb as the Gordon lads extended their collections. Hell, Jimmy Connacher even had one dating back to the 1960s, similar to the model used in the first *Pink Panther* movie. But there was still a problem. As a result of our efforts in the trading arena, we had been completely cut out of the underwriting syndicates.

These were the groups set up to distribute shares from a new issue. Obviously even a very large firm can't place all the shares of a large new issue with its own accounts, so a group of dealers form a syndicate to distribute shares among the clients. As a result of our bad manners and unruly behaviour, the Gordon lads weren't invited to join these gatherings.

The boys in the corner office had figured it out. If the establishment wouldn't let us into the underwriting agency business, then we would establish an underwriting principal, or liability, business. That is, we would buy the shares directly from the company wanting to issue new stock to the public and sell it from our hands. Sort of like the liability-trading business. Hell, we had already done liability/principal issues in the form of Wharf and Denison.

Word was out that Royal Bank was going to do a $25-million preferred share issue. The brokers had just started beating up the market for bank-preferred shares to be able to extract a rock-bottom price from Royal Bank for the new issue. The issue was supposed to be a million shares of $25 preferred. The brokers were busy trying to make bank preferreds look bad, not to mention Royal stock, and thus price the new issue at a below $24 a share to themselves.

A couple of our guys walked across the street to see John Cleghorn, who was CEO of the bank. They offered him a cheque for an amount larger than he would have received from the underwriters. They came back with the share certificate in their hip pockets. The deal was done. I can imagine the conversation over at Dominion Securities or Wood Gundy.

Reggie walks in on Winslow while the latter is practicing his putting on the priceless silk Qum carpet in his office

"Reggie, how's the Royal pref thing going?" Winslow asks.

"Haven't you heard? It's been sold."

"What? You mean we did the red herring (preliminary prospectus), the green sheet, and the prospectus all in a week and sold the issue as well? Why was I not informed? Who's running the book on that deal? He's to be congratulated. Drinks in the boardroom at four-thirty."

"Actually, we didn't sell it. The Royal Bank sold it."

"Even better, we don't have to keep a book and bother the sales staff. Who did the bank sell it to? Their depositors?"

"No, Gordon Securities, who sold it to their clients."

"The cheek! Did they offer us a piece of the deal?"

"Afraid not. You know, we didn't offer them a piece of the last Consumers Gas issue or actually any other issue that I can remember."

"Oh my god."

It would now have struck home. The mayhem created in trading was going to be repeated in the underwriting arena.

There was much jubilation in the Gordon tent that night. We felt that the economics would drive all the underwriting business our way. I was impressed, but then I had been impressed with liability trading as well and that had bankrupted us. I decided I'd have lunch with Norm Carney. He knew more about the market than I could ever hope to learn.

29

Sisyphus' Rock

NORM and I sat down to our usual plate of lamb chops and bottle of claret. When the opening salvo of martinis had been finished, but before the chops had landed, I said to Norm, "What do you think of this new gimmick? We buy the whole issue from the corporation, get a prospectus, and blow it off to the investors."

"The bought deal! How simple. How elegant. It has to be a winner. Everybody benefits, especially the clients – both buyer and issuer."

"Norm, you forgot to mention us, the vendors."

"We should do pretty good. This is better than taking positions where you buy currently trading shares from a client not knowing what the price will be in ten minutes."

Norm noted that with the market priced in eighths,* a share price moving down an eighth meant we lost money because we only tacked on seven or eight cents a share to do a trade. "Nobody shares the loss with us, but someone eats a portion of the profit should the share move up an eighth while we own it."

By now we were well into our chops.

"We can make this work in the same way we made your Denison trade work," Norm continued. "Our traders blabbed the news that we would soon be dispersing over a million shares of Denison in the market to all and sundry. The hills were alive not with the sound of music but of buyers retracting their bids. We kicked the shit out of the price, went short, sold

---

*Shares that traded at price of over $5 were marked up or down and quoted in eighths of a dollar changes, or $0.125.

a slug of naked calls,* and bought all the available puts.† The market was better dressed than a Thanksgiving turkey. If someone else had got the block of Dension, we would have been in deep shit. We believed and I guess hoped you'd get it."

Norm paused from mopping up the last of his nourishment, then said: "With the bought deal we can do the same thing. Dress the market before we go in and bid for the new shares being issued. With our position on the floor and our desk traders, the opposition won't know the depth of our pre-positioning and we can outbid anybody and make it work. We'll make a lot of money preparing the market by short-selling the shares and working the options market. Hell, we'll make money out of other firm's bought deals. We can't lose. Too bad about your job. Maybe the partners can find something else for you to do."

Norman Carney knew his stuff. He was our options trader and proceeded to dress the market before we did any big trade by selling calls against our long positions and buying puts against our shorts. If we bought twenty-five thousand Bank of Montreal shares from a client with the intention of selling it, we might sell call options (the right to buy shares from us at a set price). The sale of the calls would add to our profit margin, and if the shares fell after we unloaded them, the calls could be bought back at a discount to the price we paid for them. The put options (requiring a market participant to buy the shares from us at a set price) were bought when we were long, because they would allow us to sell at predetermined price should the market fall away while we had the share. Because of all the possible machinations in the derivatives market, Norman knew whereof he spoke.

"What the hell do you mean by that?" I asked in full moral indignation. "I'm the top-rated mining analyst in the country!"

Arrogance was not our weak suit at Gordon.

"We are now just like any other big brokerage firm," Norm said. "The irony is that we have destroyed the gold mine that existed because of the

---

*Naked calls are contracts to sell shares to investors without having the shares in inventory. It is a form of short selling.

†The speculator who sells you a put contract is required to buy shares from you at a predetermined price irrespective of the market price. Put contracts are exercised if the market price is lower than "strike," or contract, price.

old structures of fixed commissions and leisurely agency underwritings. Soon everyone on the street will be doing bought deals and liability trading, the margins will get shaved, and you'll be just overhead."

"Norm, you're nuts. Gordon is always going to need research. They can't tell when to position in a deal without some idea of real-market support. Do you expect the firm to take on a couple hundred thousand Inco onto their books without first determining if the shares are suitable?"

"Yeah. Think about the Denison deal where we bought 1.7 million shares from Dome Mines and then blew it out into the marketplace. Frank Constantini and the trading desk had a picture of what it was going to be like to sell that volume of shares and they obtained it by talking to the street. It had nothing to do with quality of earnings, the uranium market, and the long-term outlook for the company, the kind of information you would supply. It was a simple analysis of what was the appetite for the shares at the moment. Gordon doesn't need a top-ranked mining analyst at two hundred grand a year. They can get by with a monkey and feed him peanuts. You're high-cost overhead."

Norm was right – but he was wrong as well. It would take some time to see it all come out in the final play of the hands.

30

Let's Buy Wood Gundy

WHAT? you may ask. The venerable firm of Wood Gundy being purchased by a bunch of Greeks, Wops, and Jews?

Yes, Gordon attempted to buy Wood Gundy (now owned by the Canadian Imperial Bank of Commerce). How could such a thing happen?

Remember the bought deal? That's where instead of the investment dealer selling a new issue of shares as agent for the vendor, he purchases them outright as principal from the issuer and sells them to the public. That was the system introduced by Gordon to overcome the closed-shop approach of the old underwriting syndicates. With Gordon doing it and taking all the business, the old-line dealers had to get into the act, becoming players in the bought-deal market.

Then one morning, while being driven to work, the head of Wood Gundy morphed into the dentist from Owen Sound. There was an issue of British Petroleum being shown around the street, and some of the dealers were looking at doing it as a bought deal. The more the Gundy guy looked at it, the more beautiful it became. It was Pharos Industries all over again. This was too good to share with those dopes out there in the market. Let's keep as much as possible of this for ourselves, sell it to the public, and buy bigger yachts, was the attitude.

Gundy got into a bidding war for the issue and bought it. It was a big piece of change in the hundreds of millions of dollars – British Petroleum isn't going to do ten or fifteen million–dollar issues. Regrettably, as a result of a change in market sentiments, particularly for oil companies, by the time Wood Gundy got around to marketing the shares, the market was a

139

lot lower. Also, because they thought it was so good, they were reluctant to syndicate out and therefore owned a major portion of it.

It gets worse. Jim Connacher had worked at Wood Gundy and at the sight of his picayune bonus cheque in 1974 left in a huff. Now, seeing his old firm on its knees was too much for him. Some say Jim danced while going over to see his old nemesis to make them an offer of salvation. The trading desk at Gordon was already dividing up the spoils of war and letting it be known in the trading arena who could expect to be working and at what jobs once the takeover was finalized. It was only a little less degrading than going through US Immigration at the Toronto airport. At least the Gundy guys weren't strip-searched as they left their offices.

What a lot of people didn't know was that Gordon desperately needed someone like Gundy with a significant presence in the US. You may remember the name Mike Milken. He had sold junk bonds to the US savings and loans (the equivalent of Canada's old trust companies) after the US Senate Banking Committee relaxed the rules regarding the quality of securities that the savings and loans could buy. One such was Columbia Savings & Loan. It had a portfolio of junk bonds that were deeply under water. The bids for them were thin (small volumes) and at big discounts from par. When analysed, the portfolio showed that with a little patience and a return to strength in the US economy, the bonds would be good quality once more. To make things better, many of them were convertible into the shares of the issuing companies. To make things even better still, the interest payments of those debentures not in default meant the portfolio could be bought with a positive carry. The interest earned far outpaced the current cost of borrowing in the short-term market.

The S & Ls could not sell the junk bonds for anything like what they had bought them for. When depositors came calling for withdrawals at places like Columbia, there was not enough money or saleable securities in their portfolios to provide payment. The US government, which was going to be stuck for the deposit insurance in any case, set up an organization to provide an orderly dispersal of these securities. US taxpayers were going to get stuck for the bill. But as one of the Gordon partners said, "They're not our taxpayers," so Gordon made a bid for the Columbia portfolio.

This caused much angst among such firms as Oppenheimer, Goldman Sachs, and Lehman Brothers. Until the entry of Gordon into the salvage operation, there had been one seller, the US government, and a few buyers, the large US brokerages. As you can well imagine, the presence of one vendor and a few buyers does not make for an efficient market. Also, the knowledge that the vendor is not profit motivated but results oriented meant that these salvage operations were being priced low.

Gordon had deep pockets in the form of Brascan to back their foray into the junkyard. The US dealers were appalled that someone was willing to offer a fair price for what they had been buying at bargain-basement levels. The US dealers were quick to point out that if you sold a large portfolio of convertible junk bonds to a foreigner, the next thing to expect would be the Japanese buying Rockefeller Center and the Arabs picking up US ports on the cheap. Someone had to defend the country's honour and protect those uppity Canadians from paying too much for Columbia's inventory. The fact that Gordon was offering cash, with the deal structured any way you wish, was not allowed to prevail.

Had Gordon merged with Wood Gundy, the latter company's long and strong presence in the US might have allowed us to pick up some of the distressed portfolios from the US government and hence provide the American taxpayers a peck on the cheek to go along with the screwing they were experiencing at the hands of the US dealers. But it was not to happen. After the Gordon traders and corporate-finance guys finished applying the boots to their counterparts at Wood Gundy, they would have merged with a bucket shop rather than put up with Gordon.

It was a match that any wedding arranger would have been proud of. Gundy had a magnificent retail and bond operation. Gordon had control of the trading floor (at fifteen percent, their dollar and share volume was the largest on the exchange) and was a killer institutional operation. There was fear on the street. If this merger went ahead, Gordon would rule the Canadian investment scene. The Lake Ontario Navy, also known as the Royal Canadian Yacht Club, and the other yacht clubs would be decimated. Most of the Gordon guys didn't sail; their only pursuit was the ownership of fancy cars. If the deal went ahead, there would be a glut of mansions and yachts while the waiting list for new Ferraris would lengthen by decades.

The establishment firms didn't have to worry about the deal going through. There were other forces at work – primarily the fact that at Gordon we never missed an opportunity to miss an opportunity. We spent months searching for opportunities too good not to be missed. The take-over of Wood Gundy was one such. Jim Connacher soft-soaped the upper management and convinced them that this was a merger of equals, of which they were the greater equal, though bankrupt. Jim's aw shucks act always convinced someone to part with something, and he had convinced Paxton, Ed King, and the lads at Wood Gundy that they were taking us over. Sort of. They were actually going to part with their whole firm.

Now we did have a lot of free capital, because we had turned down participating in the privatization of British Petroleum, which is what Wood Gundy had not done. But still, with the size of Gundy it was not going to be free. They had really stubbed their toes and a massive bailout was needed.

Neil Baker went over to see his former protégé at Brascan, Jack Cock-well, and the necessary hundred or so million shortfall on our part was to be forthcoming from Brascan. Everybody was salivating at Gordon and Brascan. There would be no Ferraris left for anybody else in Canada. After this deal, the Gordon guys would buy them all. The Brascan guys would take over the Columbia Savings and Loan portfolio and thereafter own a major portion of mid-tier USA. They would be the Kings of Bay Street.

The Gordon Capital corporate-finance lads – in the form of Peter Hyland – and the stock-trading department through Frank Constantini were so enraptured that they strolled over to the Gundy offices and made it clear to the brethren there who was going to stay and who was walking the plank. I suspect the paramount indignity came when Peter announced that he wanted to move some walls for an office larger than that of the head of Gundy, Ed King. The Gundy guys were mortified. If two Gordon Capital partners could start thinning the ranks before the merger, how safe was any Gundy employee, partner, or director?

The prospect of a reign of terror equivalent to that of the French Revolution was more than the Wood Gundy stalwarts were willing to accept. They started looking around for alternatives. Having had a marriage proposal from Gordon Capital, Gundy was already looking better and a bailout was soon arranged. We at Gordon made it impossible to consummate the marriage by abusing the bride before the wedding could take place.

This was not the kind of news that anyone wanted circulating in the financial markets. If Gundy could fail, who couldn't? If a bunch of ethnics could take a run at Gundy, who was safe?

31

The Winners' Ellipse

THERE was no question we were on a winning streak. Prior to the attempt to buy Wood Gundy, we had become a force to be feared. But there were problems. The partners were spending as if they owned more than one gold mine. There were constant debates concerning what to put money into, such as bond-trading schemes and politicians. Yup, politicians. They are readily available and thus very reasonably priced.

Jean Chrétien was in the wilderness. The non–Natural Ruling Party – aka the non-Liberals – was in power temporarily under Brian "trust me" Mulroney. Jean, as leader of the Natural Ruling Party, being unemployed, was running low on golf balls, so a piece of him was offered to us at a measly knock-down price of $50,000 a year. The deal was so good that we and a merchant-banking firm immediately snapped up a piece of the next prime minister for that price, knowing that once he returned to power an intravenous attachment to Canada's treasury would be connected and we, along with the ad-agency boys, would be on it.

Jean would come down from Montreal about once a month or so on Fridays,, and we would have a sandwich with him and each of us put in our plug for the head of some board or other and then dash off to have lunch with a client and do some real business. Anyone who stayed longer than it took to eat three sandwiches ended up with a government gig and, as I am told, some good business directed to the firm when Chrétien was returned to power. So he was, for a while, a "consultant" to Gordon Capital and part of the winners' circle.

In our case, the winners' circle was really a winners' ellipse. After the many innovations that Gordon had brought to the investment business, it was considered *de rigueur* to say you were, had been, or would be, part of the firm. For example, Don Coxe, when he was director of research, instituted a report at the end of each quarter whereby the analysts explained their worst-performing recommendations. That occurred in 1984, and since then I have seen research directors, salesmen, portfolio managers, and stock messengers all claim to have initiated that kind of report.

Summer students who only worked a brief semester at Gordon embellish their current résumés with the lofty positions they held at Gordon. If the current human-resources professionals were to subtract the applicant's age from the date of employment at Gordon, they would find that the individual had been the head of sales, director, and partner of the firm beginning a few weeks after birth.

At the time, we ruled Bay Street, so everyone wanted to be onboard. Our notoriety was such that some fellow at my son's school, St. George's, had mentioned that we were the only real dominators of the Street. My twelve-year-old son, wanting to meet me for lunch, called at our receptionist's desk and asked for the King of Bay Street. Without even looking up, she replied, "Which one?"

Our winners' circle could not maintain its shape because we constantly had to bring in losers. These were girlfriends of partners or clients as well as castoffs of major clients. Remember that the firm's success was founded on acquiring a dream team of proven talent: men – yes, they were all men – who could bring in business because of their past successes. In 1986, to accommodate friends and family, we were bringing in kids under thirty years old with no track record or experience. They would stick around long enough to embarrass us or cost us some cash or grief and then move on, claiming they had been a star at Gordon Capital. In one case, one of these men assaulted a partner and then went on to become the industry's best-known pugilist and most highly disregarded trader.

What about women? you ask. Ah yes, women. Tried them. Didn't like them. When I joined the firm in 1980, one of our female traders couldn't square her trading duties while taking care of her newborn. She actually wanted to breastfeed the innocent waif while working the blotter. Another had a lip affliction. It was too often connected to a martini glass.

The Reichmanns were one of our larger clients. In the mid-1980s Canada's government was possessed with the idea of repatriating our greatest national assets. Among those were, in their opinion, our oil and gas. Never mind that these were depleting assets and their prices were currently upwardly distorted. They had to be brought back into Canadian hands. One of the oil companies that saw an opportunity to offload some over-priced assets to the overly willing buyers was Gulf Oil. They owned Gulf Canada and were more than happy to help the Canadian government facilitate a purchase at the top of the market. Mind you, the Canadian government was a little short of cash to make this purchase, having shot its bolt on buying the pieces that went into making Petro-Canada. Gulf US was not keen to take paper, because they knew, this being the top of the market, that any shares they received for their Gulf Canada stocks were bound to depreciate. So cash was king.

The Reichmanns had cash. The reason they had cash was that they had learned the secret of the market: buy low, sell high. You would be amazed by how few people can get those four words in the right sequence. The Reichmanns had used this acumen to buy real estate in New York City in 1972 when the town was going to go broke and in the eyes of most investors would be bulldozed over. Well, when you have mastered the four-word series and someone comes along offering to sell you an oil company at the top of the market, you politely demur.

But remember, Brian Mulroney and his gang of thinking machines were determined to bring the goodies home. So Neil Baker and Peter Hyland, the Gordon stalwarts, put together a scheme whereby the government would give some lucrative tax breaks to the Reichmanns if they did the deal. The proposal was discussed in Gordon's offices and refined to be unassailable by either side. The lads went to Ottawa, and the deal was consummated. When the news broke, the investment world was agog. The deal just didn't make any sense. It did if you knew all the details, however, but they were unavailable to the public.

Then one morning Diane Francis's column in the *Financial Post* described how the deal had been structured and what benefits were to accrue to the participants as bestowed by the government.

We were all frog-marched individually into Jim Connacher's office, where with eyes closed to slits and teeth gritted, he asked, "Do you know or have you ever known Diane Francis?"

I was cocky enough to ask if he meant in the biblical sense and got thrown out of the office. But I was intrigued enough to want to meet her. She did not admit to having a mole in our offices, so I had to believe that she had deduced the deal from putting together what she could glean from loose lips in Ottawa, of which there is always a plethora.

The lunch at La Fenice restaurant on King Street proved to be less than enlightening. After two bottles of good Barolo, I still had no answers. Diane glanced at her watch and said, "Three o'clock. Got to run. Column to write."

I, on the other hand, was wondering if the elevator ride to the fifty-fourth floor of the TD building would be a wise undertaking, considering the state of my head, stomach, and liver.

I still had no name.

Connacher was furious, because one of our best clients now regarded us as untrustworthy. We took a hit on future business, and there was, besides, a sense of anger, the scent of betrayal. Someone in the firm was blabbing our most intimate secrets. No one noticed the smiling face of one of the ladies at the firm. As a result of her membership in the Amalgamated Brotherhood of Sistership, anyone who could say "female eunuch" without chuckling could get all the latest on what the misogynists at Gordon had most recently undertaken.

Those without functioning mammalia need not apply.

IV

PAYING THE TOLL

32

An Emergency Nose Job

ALL this action was taking its toll on me. I developed polyps on my vocal cords that made speaking difficult and made me sound like Peter Lorre. This had me, not to mention the clients, somewhat frightened. When hearing me on the phone, they didn't know if they had been called by a Mafia don or were receiving an obscene phone call. I couldn't speak above a whisper.

When I was working for Kennecott I had a wonderful health plan that covered everything, immediately. Upon leaving, I was reminded of the story of the death of Sir Arthur Lucas, the English mogul who ran the company that supplied the electrical bits such as headlights to most of the cars built in the UK. As some of you who have owned Jaguars will recall, the electrical systems were their weakest points. On his death bed Sir Arthur called over his wife and told her that he had a very important life-and-death message for her ears only. As she bent close he whispered into her ear, "Don't drive in the dark, dear." When I left Utah one of the recently arrived Canadian émigrés whispered in my ear, "Make sure you don't get sick up there."

I did. I developed the aforementioned polyps and found Dr. Lorne Tahrsis to remove them. My Utah friends proved prophetic, because Tahrsis was unable to perform the operation he had scheduled for me and moved on to do cosmetic surgery. I then found Dr. Peter Alberti. However, to get the operation done, I had to raise money for the laser instrument he wanted to use on my throat.

The health thing was starting to get scary. After eight operations on my throat over the space of a year, Dr. Alberti informed me that the stress of my employment was causing my illness. If I continued in the trade I would end up with vocal cords so scared as to be useless, he said. But other scary things were happening in my life. Murray Pezim was back.

33

Prospecting in the Courts

IF you are having trouble finding a mine, the best place to look is in the courts. There is an old adage in mining that the first in the bush is the prospector, followed by the drillers, and finally the lawyers. As I mentioned earlier, there was more money paid to the lawyers from the great Virginia City finds than to the shareholders.

You may remember that in the 1980s Murray Pezim was drilling some moose pasture near Wawa, Ontario. The moose pasture turned out to be underlain by one of the largest gold finds in Canadian history. It was the famous Hemlo find. Those who were too late to find their own properties resorted to the Virginia City gambit, finding a mine in a court brief, a tradition that has been adopted by Canadian mining promoters.

Murray had staked a great swath of land in the Wawa/Hemlo area, as had the Hughes–Lang promoter team. Most of that property had been vested with companies in the various promoters' stables. That only left the claims of the Williams family open for drilling. The geologist for Lac Minerals asked for, and was granted, permission to visit the drilling operation being carried on by Corona Mines, Murray's company. The geologist came away impressed, and Lac negotiated an agreement with the Williams family to explore their claims in the area. Corona chose not to get into a competition for the Williams claims.

The drilling on the acquired ground proved successful, and Lac Minerals, a mid-sized Canadian gold company, began development of the site. At this point Murray popped up and said he had intended all along to acquire the property for Corona and that Lac Minerals had gone behind Corona's back to acquire the claims. There was a slight problem with that position, however. Murray's modus operandi had always been to put the claims surrounding any of his drilling plays into different companies in order to have as many deals going as possible and hence enhance his profitability. If he had followed his usual pattern, that is what would have happened with the Williams claims. To pursue Lac Minerals on Murray's behalf alone would not have won the day for Pezim. Lac was acting on information belonging to Corona, not Murray Pezim. The latter couldn't very well claim he was impoverished, because Lac had acted on Corona's information.

Pezim therefore chose to make his case through Corona. The lawyers for Lac made the point that there was no evidence to indicate that Murray was about to break from his long-standing pattern of picking up surrounding ground for other companies in his stable. During the trial, Mr. Bonhomme,* a long-time participant in the exploration industry, testified that an approach to Mrs. Williams for her claims by a company called Hemglo had been turned down in favour of the offer of Lac Minerals and that Hemglo was acting for Murray Pezim, not for Corona. Mr. Bonhomme also stated that Pezim would have sold the claims to one of the junior companies in his stable. Also, it was clear that Corona had not pursued the purchase of the Williams claims.

For those of us in the peanut gallery, the evidence was damning to the Corona case. Corona had not expressed an ongoing interest in the Williams claims. And Murray became interested after the successful drilling had been completed. Corona had not been distressed; Murray had. Corona had no case. At the summation the judge determined that he had heard the testimony of liars. He chose to rule on the basis of giving the Williams property to the most convincing and hence best liar. Corona won the day, or should I say Murray did.

On the last day of the trial, but before the judgment, the shares of Lac Minerals went up and Corona fell. It had been concluded in the investing community that Lac would triumph, especially given that the judge would

*From the *Globe and Mail*, November 14, 1985: "However, under cross examination, Mr. Bonhomme said that, in 1980 Mr. MacKinnon was considering including the Williams claims with other property he had staked for Hemglo. He also said that, if Hemglo had acquired the Williams property the company would have optioned it to Mr. Pezim although terms had not been discussed."

see that the most convincing story came from a professional liar, a mining promoter (for as Mark Twain said, " A gold mine is a hole in the ground with a liar at the other end"). Corona won the case and ownership of the Williams Mine from Lac Minerals.

I was stunned. Everything in the case had indicated a win by Lac Minerals, so much so that I had bought a position in Lac securities. However, there were two pieces of information I should have given more weight.

One was that Judge R. Holland, when he heard auto-accident cases, was said to be prone to rule on the side of the poor little insured guy versus the big nasty insurance company. He may have perceived the same scenario in looking at little upstart Corona versus established Lac Minerals.

The other was a bet made with me by Ned Goodman that Corona would prevail. This was made about three-quarters of the way through the trial when the evidence was seemingly favouring Lac, particularly with regard to the fact that Corona had never pursued the Williams claims.

Certainly the evidence given at trial indicated that the staking and property acquisition team of Hemglo, headed by Don MacKinnon, was working not for Corona but for Murray Pezim. The belief in investing circles was that Pezim had not been interested in the Williams property and if he had been it was destined for one of his other companies.

Goodman's bet was made with such confidence that I should have realized he knew something none of the rest of the investing community did about the outcome of the case.

The fallout from this case was ongoing. It was disclosed in 1990, in a lawsuit heard by the Supreme Court of Ontario, that the Provincial Mining Recorder for that area, Ms. Audrey Hayes, had been receiving large monthly cash payments of $50,000 from a Toronto brokerage firm, totalling $800,000. This was especially odd given that brokerages don't stake mining claims. The firm passing the funds to her account was A.E. Osler, then run by Len Gaudet, who was eventually convicted of financial irregularities when Osler collapsed. The funds had been funnelled through an intermediary, a director of the now Goodman-controlled Corona Mines.

It gets worse. Documents that would have allowed a junior company that staked some of the original claims in the Hemlo area went missing from the Hayes mine recorder's office, thus jeopardizing the junior's claim to shares in Corona.

Because of these revelations there was much dampening of under silks in the nouveaux-riche class of Toronto. If the accusations of the Ontario Securities Commission and other august bodies were to be aired, there would be revelations that would destroy their reputations, not to mention assets. A man with impeccable credentials (you certainly would not offer up a scoundrel) was found to take the fall. He accepted all responsibility (after a little arm twisting and palm crossing) and his career was destroyed. Lenny Gaudet's firm , the old A.E. Osler (raised to its height by the smartest man in the world, aka Peter Hyland, sold off to Alaistair Stevens, and laid low by Lenny Gaudet), collapsed. It is difficult to fathom the amount of harm and grief caused by the greed to control a gold mine. This is an asset that won't exist in twenty years, having been depleted. The stains on people's reputations and the financial pain inflicted will outlive the mine.

What about my old nemesis Murray Pezim? He learned a valuable if late lesson. When someone volunteers to help you beat up a little guy, beware of who your ally looks to take on after the little guy is gone. As is usually the case, it's you. Yes, Murray found one of the greatest gold mines in the world. Had he left it at that he would have controlled it at his death. But a salesman always falls sway to another salesman, and Murray was sold on the idea that with a little bending of the truth, his major gold find could be made even bigger. The better salesman ended up with the bigger stake and sold Murray's mine out from under him.

What did I learn from all this? That only money can buy you injustice.

34

Three Strikes and I'm Out

THINGS were looking ghastly. I had lost money on the Lac Minerals/ Corona dispute, as had some of our clients, and my doctor was telling me I would soon be doing my presentations in sign language. It seemed that no matter how much business I brought in, I never seemed to be able to make a lot of money.

What I didn't know at the time was that the corporate-finance arm of the firm took a hefty percentage of everything that came through the door. After that, when the cost for the use of capital and other expenses were taken, there was little left to spread among the partners and the instigators of deals. Again, I should have looked at what Peter Hyland, the smartest man in the world, was doing. He had given up the position of director of research and moved to the corporate-finance department.

Don Coxe was now leading research and doing a grand job of it. But we weren't getting as rich as the newspapers would have us believe. Peter's move to corporate finance should have been a signal to me that there was no profit to be made in Gordon on the brokerage side. Peter always went where the money was.

The orientation of the shop had changed, as well. Whereas in the past the objective was to facilitate the client, the new mantra was to "do the deal." After we had successfully stolen the Royal Bank preferred–share issue from the old-line brokers, we introduced the bought deal with a vengeance. We then went on to do a $200-million new-share issue of Canadian Utilities. The bought deal, as you may remember, is where the broker buys the new-issue shares from the corporation that's seeking funds and sells these to the clients. This was much more lucrative and safer than trading shares.

I continued to write my research reports on the companies in the mining segment of the market. I was worried about the comment Norm Carney had made that I was now redundant, but I pushed it to the back of my mind. I hadn't realized and Norm did not have the heart to tell me I was an impediment to the bought deal.

That came out after I had finished a two-month examination of the metals markets and Falconbridge Mines, in the spring of 1987. It was obvious to me that Falconbridge's stock was overpriced, and I laid out why in a report. When, after two weeks, the report had not been published, I asked the head of research why. Don Coxe told me that Gordon Capital was purchasing a couple million shares from the treasury of Falconbridge for further sale to the investors. The distribution to the pigeons was being done at this time because it was the top of the market for Falconbridge shares and excerpts from my report had convinced the company's management of this. We couldn't very well have a report recommending that investors sell the shares in circulation while trying to convince them to buy new shares from us. Some of the Gordon stalwarts even suggested I rewrite the report as a buy recommendation.

Now I was in a real dilemma. My only real asset was my profession and ranking as an analyst. If I were to jeopardize my position as an analyst, I would have nothing to offer. If I stayed at Gordon, my reputation would be tarnished because of my association with an underwriting house that gave no recognition to research but just wanted to belt out product to the street. There were those in the firm eyeing my participation in the remuneration pool, saying it was unnecessary because good research was counterproductive. Why did we need a ranked analyst when all he did was write reports describing Gordon's new offerings as sale candidates? What the firm needed was unbiased research. That was the kind that was in tune with and supportive of the latest underwriting.

You have to understand the nature of the stock-distribution business. The first conundrum is, as my Greek father would say, "If this is so good, why are they willing to sell it to me?" Companies raise capital from the public to build or expand their business. If the company has a thriving enterprise and sufficient assets, it will raise the money by borrowing from the public through a debenture or bond issue. If it there is more risk in the venture than what would accommodate a loan, then a portion of the business must be sold through a share issue. But if you issue shares, you are diluting the ownership of the current shareholders, hardly a benefit to them. So in many cases where an established company comes to the market, it is out of duress.

To accommodate this, the new shares are discounted to reflect the risk. Obviously, in most cases a company coming to market with shares is not in the best interest of the existing shareholders, and the company is too shaky to borrow. Sounds like a sell candidate to me. It is a conflict of interest to have an impartial analyst at a firm that is distributing shares. This was recognized by the US Securities Exchange Commission, which after the tech-stock bubble of 2000 decided that there had to be a complete separation between underwriting and research in US investment firms.

During that tech boom, in the late 1990s, the Wall Street analysts Henry Blodget and Mary Meeker were extolling the infinite earnings capabilities of the companies whose new issues their firms were flogging. The issues immediately went to a premium after the issues were completed. Many of the companies that were financed on the basis of the "impartial research" no longer exist. The brokers selling the new shares and the corporate insiders who sold their positions to the public made fortunes. The pigeons had their wings clipped. The lads at the SEC in the US finally recognized why the British investment business was built on the separation of share distribution and share brokering.

It came down to this: The underwriting business was so lucrative and ego boosting for Gordon Capital that real research was jettisoned. They were back to the old "We own, therefore we recommend." We old-timers at Gordon, refugees from large firms, now found ourselves back where we started, at large firms.

In its early days the Brendan Wood employment–search firm – okay let's just call them headhunters – would look for a person to hire in the investment industry by phoning around Bay Street to see who was highly thought of, say, in research, trading, or sales. This then led to a formalized survey that was done annually. In the 1987 survey I could see that Gordon's personnel were slipping, overall, while I was holding steady. If I stayed at Gordon I would be damned by association and my ratings would fall.

The vibes around the firm were that I was expensive. Better to hire a monkey and feed him peanuts. To make things worse, my doctor was back to playing star wars in my throat with his laser. I was in a serious jam.

I knew Gordon couldn't just let me go, because that would be a black eye for the firm. The good junior analysts were already leaving. Letting me go would be a sure signal to the industry that the firm had given up its research/trading function for stock distribution and that their research was worthless.

But I also couldn't just quit, because I would take a screwing on the value of my participation in Gordon and there would be no severance.

One thing was sure. I had to get out.

Once again I turned to the smartest man in the world. I was sitting at my desk when Peter walked by. It struck me that if he were in my situation he would make Gordon fire him. My dilemma was how to do that. I threatened Jim Connacher with a thrashing in the bar at the 54th Restaurant over the picayune payout I was getting on the business I was bringing in. That was unsuccessful, because Jim ducked and directed me to Bob Fung in the corporate-finance department. I then offered to put out *his* lights for "clipping" my part of a deal. He wouldn't step outside, but I waited for my pink slip all the same.

Nothing.

It became obvious that internal matters were not going to bring the boys to the table. After all, for them a black eye was better than a big payout. There had to be a better form of embarrassment. I knew if word got out that the Gordon Capital research guys were looking around for other employment, the firm would try to stop it. So I went to see one of Jim Connacher's friends, Lou Emiloy, about a job. He reported back to Jim and I had my offer on the table by the time I returned to my office. In May 1987 I was gone.

35

Scoundrels Anonymous

WORKING in the financial markets makes it difficult to determine if you are a scoundrel or just one of the boys. What amount of transgression requires that one acquire a mentor and attend the weekly meetings of Scoundrels Anonymous? It was a Greek who got me considering the degree of my scoundrelling, or more accurately described, an Australian Cypriot, Chris Kyriacou. I helped him establish the First Toronto operation, which was meant to be a mining merchant bank. It was well known on Bay Street that I had thrown in my lot with a bunch of wild Aussies. As a result the investment community saw me as the true source of all things Australian.

I had kept my trading account at Gordon but was often surprised how my trades would often generate substantial market activity. It was as if I were being front run. Front running describes the trading done by the broker in advance of filling your order. So let's say you are a director of Stelco and you call and ask your broker to sell ten thousand of your Stelco shares at $25. What you might see is an ensuing flood of selling. This would occur as the trading desk or the salesman with whom you placed the order determined that if an insider was selling stock, he should, as well.

I was pretty sure some front running was going on but I couldn't prove it. However, knowledge is power. Get even, don't get angry. These are two very good pieces of advice. After having done a few trades and watching how the market reacted, I acted on my suspicion that a little hanky-panky was going on. I opened an account at Thomson Kernaghan to place my trades a little more discreetly. Then the news started to circulate that the

Macquarie Bank of Australia was going to take a major equity position in the Bank of British Columbia. People began to quiz me, as the Canadian pipeline to Australia, on the veracity of this rumour.

The proposition made no sense because the Australians would not be able to own a controlling position in the bank. But it was known that the bank was for sale. I bought five hundred shares of Bank of British Columbia preferred shares at Gordon for $22 apiece. They had been discounted by virtue of fears about the dividend continuity. After my purchase I saw trading skyrocket in the shares and the price move to $25 and an eighth. So I shorted five thousand shares at my Thomson Kernaghan account the day after the shares paid their dividend. I then sold my Gordon position and inquired if it was possible to borrow stock to go short. By the end of the month, and three-quarter-million share trades later, the preferreds were back to $22 a share.

Now there's a moral dilemma for you. Was I scoundrel for allowing people to think I was in possession of inside information that they were going to act on? Is it immoral to front-run front runners? Should I have told people who assumed I was an insider that I was not? I tried to feel guilty as I glanced through the travel brochures looking for ways to spend the $15,000 I had made.

36

They Had Me by the Throat

I had left Gordon and joined First Toronto, but the throat problems kept cropping up. The conclusion of my surgeon, Dr. Peter Alberti, was that with all the trading and quasi investment–industry exposure I was into, I hadn't really left the Street. Alberti insisted on exile.

He had attributed the need for thirteen operations on my throat to the stress of the investment business and suggested I find something quieter. I asked if giving up a seventeen-year career in the investment business as a result of health problems would garner his support for some form of disability compensation. He demurred. The doctor was of the opinion that I was too rich to be disabled, notwithstanding that I couldn't work in my chosen profession. I immediately realized that I had once again made a career-damaging choice. I had found a great surgeon but one who had a strange sense of social justice, believing that only the poor could be disabled.

The doctor had scared me enough about the dangers of the investment business to my throat and health that I didn't dare read the *Wall Street Journal* or *Financial Times*. I kept my eyes downcast when walking past the brokers' offices. I had sworn to stay away from anything that might involve the buying or selling of shares. I had even given up cigars and demon drink to save my voice,

But I was weak.

You may remember that I mentioned Randy Wood early on as the headhunter who had lured me into the offices of Deacon Hodgson after I left Ames. When he learned that I had left Gordon, he contacted me as a prospect for another headhunting project. He was heartbroken to hear that I would not be revisiting the investment business as an analyst. I noticed, during this discussion, that Randy was undertaking a new venture. He was starting a company to do what he called investor relations. This was an idea in its infancy, one not highly regarded by the public-relations industry, because they didn't understand the relationship between investors, speculators, and the companies that pursued them for investments. I decided to leave First Toronto and join Randy Wood in his new venture.

It was late 1987 and the only device for mass communication was the fax machine. If you wanted to, you could call a list of people by phone and offer them some information. Large corporations and speculative startups didn't know how to get their message out to the public. Randy knew there was a market for this kind of communication. This was one of my pursuits as a mining analyst: getting investment information into the right hands. It was a marriage made in heaven. I knew the type of information that could move share prices, and Randy knew the entire Toronto investment community, having helped many of the retail and institutional salespeople find employment throughout the years.

We started Bay Street Marketing and couldn't believe our success. We had CIBC, Deprenyl Pharma, and even American Barrick as clients. The Barrick saga on its own proved an interesting story.

Gary Last owned a small resource company called American Barrick. It had a collection of oil and gas participations and a small cash flow. At the time it was difficult to get investors enthused about oil and gas, so he sold the company to Peter Munk, who then loaded it up with some marginal gold companies, including the old Jerome Gold Mine in Ontario.

Excuse me if I digress for a minute. The Jerome name brings back an interesting piece of history. Prospectors throughout time have named their discoveries after famous mines, hoping that some of that past glory will rub off on their find. The original Jerome mine is not far from Phoenix. It was first operated as a silver deposit by the Indians, then as a copper deposit by the Spaniards.

Believing that it had been worked out, it was deserted until the Canadian geologist "Rawhide Jimmy" Douglas began to explore it on the behalf of some New York interests. He found a deep bonanza, which was named after one of the investors, a New York Lawyer named Jerome. The Jerome

Mine made Mr. Jerome fabulously wealthy. As was the custom of the times, he decided to buy, for his daughter, Jennie, a nice duke, prince, or some other form of destitute European aristocracy. He found a descendant of the Duke of Wellington who had fallen on hard times. That was Randolph Churchill. He married Jennie, lived off the Jerome millions, and sired a son by Jennie named Winston. Yup, that Winston Churchill. All bought and paid for by a mine in the hills of Arizona.

Munk did not have the Jerome millions working for him when he bought American Barrick and changed its name to Barrick, but he did have Adnan Khashoggi, the famous Saudi arms dealer. We lost the Barrick contract because Khashoggi was a bigger draw than anything we could provide. The other clients more than made up for that loss. Randy Wood had by this time begun demanding stock options from the companies we would be promoting (the CIBC declined) and the money rolled in.

The question of insider trading arose again. Was it "material" insider information that a company had approached Bay Street Marketing for investor-relations services? That was tough to call, because "material" was defined as likely to influence the price of a company's shares. Investor-relations efforts could not always be depended on to raise a share price. So if we bought shares in company X knowing that the price might move, was that insider trading? Was the information "material"? I still don't know the answer to that one.

The most impressive show we did was for Morty Shulman, the doctor who had made a fortune buying a short position in some Toronto Stock Exchange–listed warrants and then demanding that the short sellers deliver. Morty had developed a sad disease, Parkinson's. But being a feisty guy, he researched for a palliative outside the conventional realm of treatments. He found that the state drug company in Czechoslovakia had developed a drug for his affliction that suppressed the symptoms and allowed the stricken to lead an almost normal life. The only problem was that the drug had been developed by the Communists, a name regarded at the time with the same horror as terrorist today. We of NATO, NORAD, and all other things saintly weren't going to have anything to do with drugs produced within the Evil Empire or Axis of Evil or some such other unholy alliance. Problem was, the drug worked.

Morty was well known in the investing community, having written books on finance and been a successful investor over the decades. It was also well known that he had Parkinson's. He had been seen twitching his way along the canyons of finance while trying to lead a normal life. We therefore decided to rent an auditorium for Morty's presentation on the merits of his company, Deprenyl, and its blockbuster drug of the same name. We were turning people away from the door with a full house and standing room only when Morty walked quietly onto the stage, symptomless. He didn't have to say a word. The crowd broke into applause then and again after the stock moved onto higher ground the following morning.

That was a turning point for Bay Street Marketing, as well. We were now being noticed by the big public-relations firms. Overtures were made to us, but Randy wanted to remain independent. When the big firms saw they couldn't buy their way in, they started to develop their own efforts. It was slow and tedious for them because the basis of the business was having a large and accurate "book" of brokers broken down into preferences. You could really annoy a broker by sending information on a company that he would never consider. So sending information on a speculative mining stock to a blue chip broker and meeting invitations to a speculative shooter for a bank presentation could ruin your business. I figured it would take them a decade to have the kind of book we had, but also recognized that it was inevitable.

I had been with Randy a year when that old demon of stockbroking was starting to gnaw at me. I started reading the financial papers again. A sure sign that I was going to fall off the wagon.

37

Replay

THE investment business is addictive. The flow of information is overwhelming and the people astounding. When you arrive at your office in the morning, you know that the form of your business will be different from the day before yesterday. Any number of events in the world can influence share prices, and there is always something happening somewhere.

To interpret and understand those events, not to mention explain their effect on markets to clients, requires intelligent, knowledgeable people, of which there is not an overabundance.

You also know, when you start your day, that the people who surround you will be bright and funny. Yes, funny. Arthur Koestler, the famed writer, pointed out in his book *The Act of Creation* that humour is a mark of intelligence and intelligence is the need for creativity.

So who would not want to work in the investment industry?

André Desaulniers, who at the time had effective control of McNeil Mantha, a Montreal-based investment firm, had approached me. I knew that having me on the roster of a firm was the kiss of death, but McNeil had the support of the Caisse de dépôt, effectively the Canada Pension Plan of Quebec. How could they fail?

It was now 1988, and Gordon had not fallen of the rails or appeared ready to do so. I therefore figured that the Doulis curse had run its course. The other factors affecting my decision were that my throat problem had not reoccurred and I could see the limits of the investor-relations business.

So in 1988 I went over to McNeil as a director and partner, including letterhead – the full-blown deal. Over at Gordon Capital, as it was now called, the lads felt pretty smug, as well. They had control of the trading floor and big bucks backing their bought deals. Everything had now been subjugated to the purchase of new share issues and pumping them out into the market. Gordon's research was regarded by anyone still reading it as a sales tool of the underwriting arm. You could tell which companies Gordon would be bringing to market by what was being written up in the research department. Although the lads were doing well, they were still asking the question, "When am I going to be rich?"

There seemed to be an immense amount of money passing through the corporate-finance department but not a lot that ended up on pay stubs to people who owned the firm, the partners.

38

Olympic-class Front Running

IN 1989 I was feeling pretty smug over at my perch at McNeil. We had a nice little institutional brokerage business going, the backing of the Caisse de dépôt, and a good retail operation. It was like being back at my first firm, A.E. Ames, but now the names that seemed out of place on the letterhead were the likes of Harris, Mathews, Reid-Jones, and anything sounding too Anglais. I got home at decent hours and even got to have holidays with my family.

The years to 1989 were golden for Gordon Capital, though the partners still could not understand why they weren't really rich. Then in February 1989 the first aroma of something rotten under the trading desk blotter started to waft through that firm's office building. It seemed there were some very soiled blotters around. To make things worse, the ever-present nose of the Ontario Securities Commission had noticed the smell.

The blotter is an anachronism referring to the ledger that English brokers used for recording their trades. The foulness of the Gordon blotter was that the trades that were recorded either didn't take place, were done after the closing prices were known, or were done with the knowledge that a large client was taking a position.

It all started in 1979 with Michael Biscotti, the head trader at Dominion Securities, who was dazzled by the size of the profits to be made if he could trade with the knowledge he had of client intentions and underwriting activity. There was a slight problem. By the rules of the industry, he was precluded from having a trading account in which he or his firm could trade on inside information. Biscotti's solution to this dilemma was simple:

open the account with a front man. For this purpose he chose a real-estate developer by the name of John Micallef and had him open an account in his name at a low-profile brokerage. Biscotti was to share in half the profits from the account.

The Micallef account proved to be a big winner. What it needed was access to more inside information. It's fine to know which of your clients are coming into the market to buy or sell and front running* them, but if you knew the trading intentions of other firms' clients, you could become even richer.

Biscotti had a relative and that relative was Frank Constantini, the head trader at Gordon Capital.

The trading of large blocks of stock is an art. Look at the situation where a pension fund has decided they want to sell fifty thousand shares of Microsoft at $35. They are going to sell it as the entire block only. To keep a tag end would be counterproductive. The fund approaches Gordon Capital with the order. The trader looks at the market and sees the bid is for one hundred shares of Microsoft at $35.25 and offered at $35.50.

No problem? Big problem. There is no bid for fifty thousand shares. So the trader makes inquiries and finds he can dredge up orders for a block of twenty thousand shares from one buyer and twenty-five thousand from another. If he does the transaction he will be left with five thousand shares. This will go into the firm's inventory and be fed out into the market.

But wait a minute, how are you going to post a "cross" (a transaction where the broker acts as both buyer and seller) at $35 when the market price is $35.50? The trade has to be done within the confines of the market price. The buyers and sellers of the blocks won't move, so you move the market price. In this case you sell stock to the small bidders until the price is knocked down to $35. Then you post your large cross on the tape.

What about the tag end? Oh, instead of going into the firm's inventory, we'll just sell that to my cousin at the other firm. As soon as the price rebounds after our Gordon selling blitz ends, the tag end can be sold at a profit of $.50 per share when the Microsoft price rebounds to $35.50. The

---

*Front running is the process of placing an order in advance of your client. If you know that your client is willing to buy a hundred thousand shares at prices up to $70 and the stock is trading at $68, why not buy a little for yourself before the price moves up? Why not? Because it is illegal.

"B" inventory at Gordon was having a tough time making money. Biscotti was having a banner year.

In my days at Gordon, we would keep a piece for ourselves when we did a large block such as the Denison block. If you are in the position of having "dressed" the market down, why not take advantage of it and sell your piece later when the market moves up? With the arrival of the Biscotti–Constantini partnership, however, there was little of that any longer. It was sort of front running but more accurately should be called back running.

The other consideration was that the more business Biscotti and Constantini could do for their firms, the more of a rake-off would be available for them. What is the customary method of encouraging the right outcome for oneself? Bribery has always worked in the past. So the two traders started bribing traders at other firms. David Orton at Canada Trust was sold new issues after the distribution had been completed and the success of the undertaking known. If the recently issued shares were to open tomorrow at a premium to the issue price, then Orton was sold a block at issue price, which he would flip into the market at the premium the next day.

Some of these trades were done without money ever having been posted. The same was done with the trader at National Trust, Rob Baird. We're not talking chump change here. The Orton account benefited to the extent of $240,944 between June 2, 1982, and February 18, 1987, from trading with Frank Constantini.

When the OSC ruling came down, the Gordon partners should have had recognized one of their speed bumps on the shortcut to wealth. Bribery costs money. Sure, Gordon was the largest trader on the Toronto Stock Exchange in both dollar and share-volume terms, but it didn't come cheap. What should have been ending up in the partners' pockets was being siphoned off to Biscotti, Orton, Baird, and Constantini, not to mention the unmentioned.

The other catastrophe was the loss of Constantini. But first, let me explain the order process for the institutional block business.

The Gordon salesman convinces the portfolio manager at The Major Pension fund that the time has come to buy Royal Bank shares. Major Pension's trading desk probably has a direct phone line to Gordon's trading desk, as do many other institutional clients trading in large volumes.

Constantini picks up his phone line from Major Pension, accepts the order, and then looks at his block list and if he is lucky finds that one of his other clients has a block of Royal for sale. It may be more or less than the fifty thousand shares that Constantini is trying to buy.

Let's say Superior Pension Fund is showing seventy thousand for sale. Constantini now has to find a buyer for the other twenty thousand shares or convince Major Pension to buy the whole thing. Then comes the question of price. Constantini, once having convinced Major Pension to buy it all or having found a buyer for the tag end, now has to get some agreement on price. Once having everybody onside for volume and price, Constantini calls and has the floor trader dress the market up or down to the price he needs to post the trade, and the floor trader announces the cross once that price has been achieved. Whew!

The cross is the best trade a desk trader can do because he has the knowledge of who the potential seller of more stock is and who the buyers are. Also, he gets for the firm the spread or commission on both sides of the trade. But as you can see, a great desk trader has to be able to cajole both sides of the transaction to an agreed price and have the technical skill to dress the market. If he isn't working on a cross, then the counter party is a desk trader at another brokerage.

Although Frank Constantini had done a great job in preparing an understudy, John O'Sullivan, there was no one to replace Frank. As well, the clients were incensed to find that Frank had been colluding with Biscotti for years in front running and "Hillary trades" to obtain business. The bombshell on Bay Street left a big hole in the trading business. The clients didn't know how deep the rot had penetrated and at which firms. Although the picture painted by the Ontario Securities Commission was one of a few rogue traders working in concert, there was the fear that other brokerages like Gordon had poor oversight, which would mean similar events could occur.

Millions of dollars were siphoned off by these efforts and it came out of the client's and the firm's pockets. Trading is a zero-sum game in that what one client loses, another gains. If someone steps in the middle, then that bit has to come out of the client's or the firm's pocket. I was not at Gordon when the news broke, but I began to realize why I wasn't rich. I may have been able to outfox the mining promoters and investor-relations firms peddling their wares, but I was a neophyte when it came to the machinations of the brokerage firms.

The level of disclosure to the firm's participants at Gordon had declined steadily from 1980 when the capital position was circulated at day's end. No one except Hyland, Baker, and Connacher knew to what extent the firm was profitable and where the profits were going. As I look back, I am astounded at how naïve I was even after spending time with two firms prior to going to Gordon. I should have learned that in the investment business you don't get what you earn, you get what you can. But then by being on Bay Street in the first place, I had made a bad turn. I was on the wrong street.

Working underground one often encounters raise miners, men who mine vertically above their heads. Each day they advance twenty-four feet and hence have to climb that many feet further to their work stations. I have seen raise miners start their shifts by climbing three hundred feet vertically to their drill platforms. Needless to say, these men are beyond good physical fitness. A bar fight with one or two of these guys was a foregone victory for them with their opponents scattered about the floor like voodoo dolls. After the Securities Commission order suspending trading for Constantini and the realization of the costs the business was incurring, the Gordon partners looked as if they had encountered a room full of drunken, ornery raise miners. They had no sooner picked themselves up from the floor and adjusted their Gucci ties than a rematch was called.

39

The Creature from the Dark Lagoon

GORDON Capital hired Peter Bailey as a compliance officer in August 1989. The firm had pledged itself to stick to the straight and narrow. Like St. Augustine, they were going to become virtuous. But also like St. Augustine, there was to be a delay. Until 1993, to be exact, when the OSC investigated the two men involved with Gordon, Eric Rachar and Patrick Lett, and banned them from trading.

Then one day, disguised as just an ordinary bond trader, came a life form that was going to devour all of the firm's capital. This creature did to Gordon Capital what a vampire does in sucking the life blood out of a big fat juicy human.

A whiz kid named Eric Rachar came to the firm and convinced Jim Connacher that if you bought long-term provincial bonds you could pay for them with the funds you made by shorting equivalent-term Government of Canada bonds.

Let's look at a ten-year Province of Ontario bond. It might have a 5.1 percent coupon and sell at $990 to yield 5.5 percent. A Government of Canada bond of the same specs might sell for $1,000, because of the higher quality and lower risk of the bond. So if you sell the Government of Canada bond short at $1,000, you can cover the cost of the provincial bond you buy at $990. And the interest that you as the shorter must now pay is covered by what you earn on the provincial and by the recapture over time of the discount on the provincial. But remember, you made more on the sale of the Government of Canada short at $1,000 than what it cost you to buy the provincial at $990. The interest is almost a wash because the coupons are identical. You still have money left over – $10 per bond, to be exact.

Pretty slick. However, to make it worthwhile, you have to do it in the hundreds of millions of dollars and that usually means using margin. Margin is the borrowing of money to buy securities. If your client is a quasi-bank, such as the old National Trust, you need only put up a few percent of the amount of money you are borrowing on their behalf. There was another ringer. That $10 difference was not earned in total until the provincial matured in ten years. It sounded so good that Connacher made Rachar a shareholder and director of Gordon Capital. It took Rachar a year to destroy the firm.

Rachar's counterpart to these trades was a man named Patrick Lett, working under the name of Trafalgar Capital Management Coporation. The account for Trafalgar was at National Trust, and the impression was given that it was National Trust's account and therefore subject to the lower-margin requirements accorded to near banks. Now let's look at the trade. To finance this you need the $10 you took out of the trade and the margin. When the provincial bond is redeemed, you will get $10 more than you paid for it, which is part of your yield. But that's ten years out. Rachar was doing the trades and paying himself a bonus based on the $10 received today. At one point Rachar had $1.1 billion in play, all backed by phony Citibank Certificates of Deposit and excess margin. So much money was created that Rachar gave Lett $2.1 million to buy a house.

Eventually it was discovered that $120 million or thereabouts of Gordon's capital was missing. As well, the firm was under-capitalized. Much more money was required as margin because the client was not National Trust, a major financial institution, but a storefront called Trafalgar, and Gordon didn't have the money to put up for the margin shortfall. To make things worse, the certificates of deposit lodged for collateral on the original money to do the trade were not backed by securities as claimed but were un-collateralized notes.

You could hear the cheering all over the investment community. Some members of the WASP men's clubs were actually awakened by it. They finally had something on that damned upstart Irishman and they wouldn't rest until the scoundrel was properly dressed down. Wait a minute, I can hear you say, Connacher didn't do anything. He and his partners were the victims. Rachar was the culprit. Well, that's just it, the chinless lads in the blue pinstripe suits said. We can get Connacher because he didn't do anything while the firm was under-capitalized because Rachar had misused the funds. Huh? It took fifteen months for forensic accountants to figure out how the scheme was exercised, and it took the OSC about fifteen minutes to decide on suspending Connacher for three months.

But it gets worse. Because Gordon did not apply to its insurance company within the required time from when the fraud was discovered, the firm did not benefit from insurance. They were broke.

The smartest guy in the world was gone, having left before Rachar worked his magic. When you look at what Rachar was doing, you see the bare bones of what in the next few years was to become the hedge fund industry. And we have all seen where that has led: Long Term Credit, the first mega hedge fund, almost collapsed the US financial system; Portus ran off with the money; and Amaranth imploded.

The really smart guys in the financial business know that there is no free money in the system. The Gordon guys, however, knew that they were the Kings of Bay Street. Anything they touched would turn to gold. There were some great prices on used Ferraris for a while.

40

Mayday! Mayday!

THE call went out at Gordon. Somebody or something had to save the firm. While it may no longer have been the investor's best friend, at least it kept the other bandits honest. If Gordon disappeared, the collusion on underwritings – the old syndicates – would be back. Something resembling the fixed-commission scheme might be reinstated. Scary times. Buddy, could you spare me a hundred million?

Well actually, yes. Brascan, along with one of the banks, came to the rescue once again and refinanced Gordon. But would you put as much as a hundred million into the hands of some guys who had just blown that much? No, not unless you had some control. So the lenders brought their own guy, Davidson, in to run things. His was not an easy chore. If he left too much leeway to Connacher, he might find himself short a few million. If he put too tight a bridle on him, the amount of business to be done would diminish. The new guy was cautious. He hadn't got this far by taking chances. So he handcuffed Connacher and all the other Big Swinging Dicks. There were not going to be any mistakes on his watch.

But mistakes are what the investment business is made of.

Bernard Baruch, the famous financier of the first half of the twentieth century, got his major start by making a mistake. He short-sold shares in Anaconda Copper, expecting a fall in the copper market. But he did so just before Passover, a big Jewish religious holiday. His mother insisted that he not work during Passover but spend the day at home with her. Foolishly, Baruch agreed and sweated through the day wondering if his position was such that he could cover it and make a slight trading profit.

Most of his capital was at risk in this trade and he was not there to watch the events unfold. He found, on his return to work later in the week, that while he was away from his desk Anaconda had opened weaker and then plummeted. Had he been there, he would have prematurely bought back the falling shares early on to lock in his small trading profit. As it turned out, by inappropriately going short over a holiday when he couldn't work, he made a fortune.

By taking away Gordon's ability to take any risk, its potential to make any return was shut off. All that remained was a shell company. In saner times, brokerage firms were sold at book value: the difference between the value of the assets and liabilities. The reason being that the assets that made the profit on that book value were the people: assets that went up and down the elevator everyday. You can put a billion dollars on the corner of Wall and Broad Streets in New York and it will remain the same unless you have people to work with it.

Gordon had no retail operation and as such was of little appeal to the Canadian banks as a potential takeover. The banks knew that the best they could expect was to keep the BSDs at the firm in golden handcuffs for about five years. However, when looking at that alternative, they noted that if they were free to go they might start up a new entity that could terrorize the investment market once more.

There were questions. Who actually owned Gordon Capital? The appearance was that the firm's controlling partner was Jim Connacher. That was not so. Richard Li, son of the founder of the Li Ka-shing financial empire, had bought about five percent of the firm in the late 1980s and his capital was being used to finance some of Gordon's activities. As events took their toll on the firm, Richard found himself having to put up more of the capital of Gordon and hence obtaining more ownership of the firm.

It was the dentist from Owen Sound syndrome all over again and a repeat of the entry of Neil Baker into Gordon. Richard became the market with 40 percent ownership. The final outcome was that when the bleeding could not be stanched, Richard's father tried to convince the Canadian Imperial Bank of Commerce to buy Gordon. He could make this appeal, because he only owned 9.9 percent of the bank. This level of ownership, however, was not large enough to force the issue. Gordon Capital was eventually sold in 2000 to HSBC, the old Hong Kong and Shanghai Bank.

Li senior owned more of that bank than he did the CIBC. Thank God: no loss of face.

But other salvage operations had been under way earlier. As you may remember, when Eric Rachar worked his magic, Gordon's capital was destroyed. Although Gordon went to the Supreme Court of Canada, trying to sue the insurance company to get coverage for their loss, they went unpaid. After all, the primary objective of an insurance company is to not pay. However, the prime responsibility of a lawyer is to protect his client. Hey, the Gordon guys asked, where were our lawyers when we needed them? They should have protected us from either Rachar or the insurance company. The company's law firm decided to throw a bone to the Gordon partners. The lads were at least able to buy used entry-level Ferraris.

The picture, as things stood in 1991, was that Frank Constantini was in exile in the US, Peter Hyland was in happy retirement in the Bahamas, the working capital of the firm had left for sunnier climes, and a banker was learning to run the firm. The trading scandal had caused many direct lines to trading customers to grow very cold. It was not easy to do financings for clients with no distribution network, and the only people coming forward to replace the departing stars were kids and washed-out veterans.

At the same time, the so called Big Bang was occurring. Only investment people could be egotistical enough to name changes in their industry after the event that created the solar system. The Big Bang was the repeal of the Glass-Steagall Act in the US. This act was brought in during the 1930s when the investment-banking arms of many of the commercial banks were bringing about the collapse of the banks as a result of the stock-market fall of 1929. A logical way to prevent this from happening was to separate investment banking from commercial banking. However, in the 1990s the banking industry heard the five most terrifying words in the investment lexicon: "This time it is different." The act was scrapped and Bank of America, City Bank, as it was then known, and a slew of others now either bought or created their own investment and brokerage operations.

Canadian bankers never missed an opportunity to destroy shareholder wealth by copying some foreigner's financial wet dream, and therefore decided that they, too, had to get into the action. After all, didn't they practically own the industry? They provided all the capital through loans to the brokers to run their operations or as loans against the equity owned by the partners. They didn't think about the issue of who was responsible if the capital was wiped out, as it had been in Gordon's case. If a bank had owned Gordon, rather than the partners, it would have had to swallow the loss. As it turned out, the owners of the firm took the hit.

With the near collapse of some hedge funds, and the outright demise of others, the Canadian bankers began to realize how risky the investment business really was. Then CIBC took a hit on Enron for a couple of billion and the object of desire was now looking like a hag. The banks had bought all the big Canadian brokers and therefore had no one to sell to The other stumbling block was that the investment guys knew the brokerages were only worth their book value, even though they had originally sold them to the banks for multiples of up to three or four times book value. So they weren't going to pay the banks any more than book.

The only option open to the banks was to increase the restrictions on their investment bankers and squeeze their retail people for more revenue. The result was that the big producers on the retail side of the business went to the independent dealers where they got a bigger share of the "ticket": the commission generated by a trade. The bank-owned retail firms ended up with brokers who stuck to buying mutual funds with trailer fees. Trailer fees are commissions that are paid as long as the client holds the mutual fund. The commission has to keep coming in, or the broker comes to work to find his desk is gone.

On the investment-banking side, independents like GMP in Canada collected the refugees from the big firms (read banks) and these were the best and brightest. They in turn provided the ideas that the corporate leaders could use. In reality, "This time it is different" proved to be as false as usual.

There is a very strong message here. In a service industry such as a stockbrokerage, the assets come in the front door and eventually get to their desks everyday. Nobody owns the assets. As well, the customer's belief in the integrity of his service supplier is paramount. All the money that is siphoned off for the Hillary Trades, the kickbacks, and front running has to be plucked from some golden goose, and that goose is you. The client has to know that his agent is working not for his own betterment but for the clients'. Next time you call your lawyer, accountant, or stockbroker, ask him who he is working for at that moment. If it isn't you, then find someone who will work for you. After all, you're paying him.

41

Give Your Throat a Voice

IN 1989 I watched the events unfold at Gordon Capital from my secure little hideaway at McNeil Mantha and placed some bets. Let's see, I left Gordon in 1987; add five years to that and they'll be gone in 1992. If the Doulis curse of collapse five years after his departure held true, I could collect a nice little pile by betting on my inherent evil.

McNeil's position in the institutional market continued to improve. For me, life was good and I sensed none of the old problems I had encountered at Ames and Gordon. McNeil was a public company with its shares listed on the Toronto Stock Exchange, so the company was subject to scrutiny. There were no special deals for the suppliers of loans as opposed to working capital, so everyone was paid what they earned.

I was living better than I ever had. Holidays consisted of cycling from Florence to Rome, sailing the Greek coast in a chartered yacht, and skiing Zermatt in the winter. I had passed the ten-year mark with the second wife and research indicated that there was no likelihood of her soon divorcing me. But being an analyst meant you were always taking a stance on metal markets and companies and there was always the chance of being wrong. The strain of my profession was still there, because people had a lot of money riding on my opinions. There was that niggling feeling at the back of my throat. Yup. Polyps.

My old physician Peter Alberti had been drummed out of the corps for a time by the College of Physicians and Surgeons of Ontario, partly for allegedly using research funds for treatment purposes. I'm told this is as dastardly as looking into a female patient's nasal cavity without a nurse present. I had to find a new ENT guy. Luckily, Dr. Dale Brown, another competent practitioner, had taken over for Alberti. He confirmed at our first meeting that after a period of two and a half years my throat was once again infected.

"Are you smoking again?"

"No," I replied. "Lips that touch nicotine will never touch mine."

"What about booze?"

"Only wine and beer and only in strict moderation."

"I see from Peter Alberti's old chart that you are in the investor-relations business. Tell me about it."

"Actually that's outdated. I am a director at McNeil Mantha."

I could catch the drift of this conversation. He wanted to know if I was back in the high-stress brokerage business. I thought that he probably would not have heard of McNeil. Also, "director" has that laidback sound to it.

He was not quite that uninformed. "So you slipped back, despite what Alberti told you," he said. "I'll operate in a month."

He made me sound like a junkie with that "slipped back" shot. But then maybe I was. Hot new drill holes, private placements, the smell of the deal all got me salivating. I didn't want to leave the investment business. I now knew all the scams and scammers and couldn't be taken advantage of. There were people not to do business with and I knew who they were. I had started to find my way on Bay Street. It was like being in the bush. In the spring you get bitten by mosquitoes for the first couple of weeks and are in agony and then feel nothing for the balance of the season. I had been bitten, chewed, and spat out by Bay Street and I was immune – except for my throat, that is.

As I walked home that night I thought about the alternatives. I couldn't work in the investment business any longer. I could go back to the bush, but I was nearly fifty years old and the wife would be unlikely to go along with that choice.

I was happiest being alone or with one other person isolated from the madness called civilization. The woods provided that. Hell, in the 1960s I was so far back in the wilderness I didn't even know Castro had taken over Cuba until my cigar shipments stopped.

When my wife and I went cycling I had that feeling of isolation, but even more so on yachting trips. She was the best bush mate I ever had since stepping out of the woods. I just couldn't picture her doing the mosquito thing in the spring. Then it struck me. I had the answer.

When I arrived home she was deep in the kitchen.

"Sally, we're going sailing."

"Great. Where?"

"The Mediterranean."

"That's lovely. How long this time?"

"Forever."

Epilogue

SALLY and I went to sea on a forty-three-foot Hans Christian seagoing yacht, *Elifthiria* (the Greek word for freedom). I found her in Fort Lauderdale, Florida, and sailed her to the Mediterranean. Nothing is forever. When we left her for the last time, fifteen years later, we both left our tear stains on her decks for posterity. I know *Elifthiria* misses us as much as we miss her.